Rice Is Nice

108 Quick and Easy Brown Rice Recipes

By Wendy Esko
Foreword by Gale Jack

One Peaceful World Press
Becket, Massachusetts

Rice Is Nice
© 1995 by Wendy Esko

For further information on mail-order sales, wholesale or retail discounts, distribution, translations, and foreign rights, please contact the publisher:

One Peaceful World Press
P.O. Box 10
Leland Road
Becket, MA 01223
U.S.A.

Telephone (413) 623-2322
Fax (413) 623-8827

First Edition: January 1995
10 9 8 7 6 5 4

ISBN 1–882984–12–9
Printed in U.S.A.

Contents

Foreword

On Thanksgiving Day, in 1949, two events occurred three thousand miles apart that would change America's destiny. Michio Kushi set foot on American soil for the first time in San Francisco, and a baby girl was born in upstate New York. Michio went on to become the leader of the macrobiotic, natural foods, and holistic health movements, while Wendy Esko became the leading macrobiotic cook born in North America.

I first studied cooking with Wendy in 1980. I discovered macrobiotics at a seminar Michio and Aveline, his wife, gave at a church in Dallas. For several years I struggled to cook for my young son and myself. It soon became clear that I needed experienced guidance, and I enrolled in the Kushi Institute, then headquartered in Brookline, Massachusetts. Wendy was my first cooking teacher and later, in 1985, when I finished the last level of the Leadership Training Program in Becket, MA (current home of the Institute), she taught every cooking class in my course. Her food was uniformly delicious, attractive, and energizing. I remember mostly the noodle and deep-fried vegetable dishes, the seaweed casseroles, and the scrumptious desserts, but the foundation of her cooking was always brown rice.

The style of cooking that I learned with Wendy enabled me to keep my—at that time—fragile health and cope with the pressures of being a single mother. Within several years, I had remarried and with my husband, Alex, who also taught at the K.I., I spent a summer living at the Esko house in Becket. I often cooked with Wendy, pounding mochi, rolling sushi, and making other dishes together, and gradually developed my skills and confidence.

Wendy had a tribe of five children at the time (she currently has eight), so her composure and concentration in the kitchen struck me as all the more remarkable. Like Wendy—who had some Iroquois ancestry—I had some Cherokee influence on my father's side, and I

5

think this background brought us closer together, as well as helped root us in the American soil. Wendy has been a pioneer, not only in introducing macrobiotic cuisine to America, but also in shaping, developing, and adapting principles of balance and harmony to this continent's unique climate, environment, and energy flow.

Wendy has written many wonderful macrobiotic cookbooks over the years. In *Rice Is Nice*, her first cookbook devoted entirely to brown rice, Wendy shares over 100 of her best recipes with us. Here is everything from basic pressure-cooked brown rice to rice and bean casseroles, rice croquettes, rice balls, rice paella, rice porridge, and mochi waffles.

In Greek mythology, Athena, the goddess of wisdom, sprang fully formed from the Zeus' forehead. In our secular age, we no longer believe in myths, fairy tales, and the arrival of mysterious culture-bearers. But the appearance of Michio and Wendy in America—on Thanksgiving, the archetypal macrobiotic holiday—can only make one wonder whether our beautiful country is still governed by a wise Providence. I hope that you enjoy this inspired book. I know your friends and family certainly will.

Gale Jack
Becket, Massachusetts
November, 1994

Gale Jack teaches cooking at the Kushi Institute and is coordinator of the Women's Macrobiotic Society. She is the author of *Amber Waves of Grain: American Macrobiotic Cooking* (Japan Publications, 1992).

Preface

I was raised in upstate New York, where the rich soil and rolling hills are perfect for growing grains, beans, and vegetables. We lived next to a farm, and it was always a pleasure to sit on our front lawn and observe the fields of grain across the way. Our neighbors grew wheat, oats, and barley. I would watch as they plowed, planted, and eventually harvested the grain. After planting, I would watch the tiny sprouts grow into mature plants. At first the fields were light green, then slowly turned golden as the grain ripened and became ready for harvest.

I loved watching the wind blow across the fields. Grain plants are so flexible and yielding. They would bow down and spring back, reminding me of waves on the Great Lakes. It was so peaceful and calming. Often my siblings and I would walk or play hide and seek in the fields, knowing that soon our beautiful playing fields would be cut and sent off to provide food for people. The grain in the fields brought forth images of steaming bowls of oatmeal on cold winter mornings, the aroma of freshly baked breads and pastries, and the rich creamy texture of thick barley-vegetable soups.

As a child I loved to eat grains. I remember asking my mother to let me eat some of my baby brother's rice cereal. I looked forward to her barley soups and grain-stuffed cabbage dishes. On Fridays, it was rare for me to be at home for dinner. Our neighbors, who were from the South, served white rice every Friday. They knew I loved rice and often invited me to join them for dinner.

I tasted my first bowl of brown rice twenty-four years ago. I was impressed by how different it was from white rice, so chewy and sweet. One of the first things I noticed was that brown rice did not leave an aftertaste in the mouth. Rather, it seemed to make the mouth feel cleaner. Unlike white rice, which I ate without feeling satisfied,

7

brown rice was satisfying and complete. I was so impressed by the taste of brown rice that after attending a macrobiotic cooking class in 1971, I readily understood the advantages of a grain-based diet.

In 1978, my husband, children, and I journeyed to Japan. We delighted in watching rice being planted in small paddies around Kyoto. I watched the wind blow across the rice fields, creating the same rolling waves I had seen as a child. We would observe the fields as if in meditation. The effect was very peaceful and calming. After seeing the rice, I felt grateful to nature and to the people who worked hard to provide our family with the grains on our table. I also felt thankful for the good health these foods had given us.

Along with cooking for my family over the years, I have cooked for thousands of students and friends. I have also given many classes on macrobiotic cooking. With every pot of rice I have cooked, I experienced the same calm, peaceful energy I felt when seeing brown rice and other whole grains in the fields.

Michio Kushi has said that there are at least a thousand ways to prepare and serve brown rice. In this small book, my first for One Peaceful World Press, I present a sample of these possibilities, beginning with the most basic methods. The basic methods of cooking brown rice are like notes in a musical scale. Hundreds and even thousands of variations can be created from them. I hope you use these recipes to create your own delicious and healthful dishes.

I would like to thank everyone who inspired this book. I thank my teachers, Michio and Aveline Kushi, who pioneered the introduction of brown rice and other whole natural foods in North America, Europe, and throughout the world. I thank my husband, Edward, for helping with the manuscript, and Gale and Alex Jack for their overall guidance. I thank Bettina Zumdick for her wonderful cover illustration, and my students, children, and friends for their love, support, and inspiration.

Wendy Esko
Becket, Massachusetts
November, 1994

Introduction

"Among cereal grains, brown rice is the most balanced. Its size, shape, color, texture, and proportion of carbohydrate, fat, protein, and minerals fall in the middle of the spectrum of the seven principal grains. Rice is biologically the most integrated grain—our evolutionary counterpart in the plant world."—Aveline Kushi

Over the past decade, brown rice has become a staple in many households across North America and Europe. The health benefits of eating brown rice are now recognized by doctors and nutritionists around the world. This ancient grain is the most widely used food crop on the planet. For 2.7 billion people in Asia, rice provides 25 to 80 percent of their daily calories. In 1993, about 520 million metric tons of rice were harvested around the world, nearly all for human consumption. Although the wheat and corn crops were slightly larger, these grains are often used as livestock feed. About 90 percent of the world's rice crop is grown and eaten in Asia, the majority in China and India.

Much of the rice harvested today is processed and sold as white rice. Brown rice is a nutritionally complete whole food. White rice is not. All rice is brown until the food processors use a process called "pearling" to remove the mineral- and vitamin-rich shell or skin. White rice is mainly starch and does not contain the natural vitamins and minerals found in brown rice.

Cultivated rice, or *Oryza sativa*, is grown in standing water, or paddies, and on dry land. Low-land rice fed by rainfall

9

comprises about 25 percent of the world's rice crop, while paddy rice comprises about 55 percent. (The word *paddy* is a Malaysian term for rice growing in deep water. It also refers to "rough," or unhulled rice.) Rice is also planted on forest slopes that have been cut and burned. This type of rice is known as "upland" rice. There is a substantial difference in flavor and energy between paddy and dry land rice.

Rice is also divided into two primary strains, based on the climate of origin. More hardy rice, or *japonica*, originated in the temperate zones. Sometimes referred to as "sticky" rice, it has short wide grains that stick together during cooking. Japonica rices have a strong sweet flavor. (California short grain brown rice is an example of japonica.) They are relatively resistant to temperature changes while growing, but are sensitive to the amount and duration of sunlight. More delicate rices, known as *indica*, originated in India and are grown in the warmer, more tropical regions. Indica rices are sensitive to temperature changes, but not to light. Basmati rice is an example of indica. Several of the more common varieties of rice are described below, and are categorized into staple rices, or those recommended for regular use, and exotic, or specialty rices suitable for special occasions.

Staple Rices

Short Grain Brown Rice Short grain brown rice is the most suitable for regular use in a temperate or four-season climate. It is the smallest, most rounded, and hardiest of the main varieties of rice. Short grain brown rice contains a high amount of gluten, which is the protein factor in the rice, along with a higher concentration of minerals. It has a naturally sweet taste and a balanced proportion of minerals, proteins, carbohydrates, and fats. The recipes in this book call mostly for the use of short grain, organic brown rice. Other varieties can be substituted according to your needs and desires.

Sweet Brown Rice Sweet brown rice is higher in gluten than the other varieties of rice. It is also slightly sweeter in taste. Sweet brown rice is often used in making mochi, a sweet taffy made by pounding the grains into a thick, sticky paste. Sweet brown rice is also used to make ohagi, a soft, sweet rice patty coated with such things as roasted walnuts, sesame seeds, sweet azuki beans, or cooked and mashed chestnuts. Sweet brown rice is used in making dumplings for soup, in making cookies, crackers, and a sweet drink called amazake.

Medium Grain Brown Rice Medium grain brown rice is slightly softer in texture than short grain rice. It is lighter and not as sweet as short grain rice. Long grain brown rice is fluffy and light when cooked. It is more suitable for use in semitropical climates or in the temperate zones when the weather is hot. It makes excellent fried rice because of its light, fluffy quality.

Long Grain Brown Rice This is the lightest of the major varieties of brown rice. It has a chewier texture than long grain white rice, and contains fiber and vitamins. Long grain rice is more suitable for use in warm weather.

Special Occasion Rices

Wild Rice Wild rice, an uncultivated aquatic grass used by native Americans, is not a member of the same species as regular rice but shares similar qualities. It is used most often on special occasions or holidays. The plant is very tall and robust. Usually the grains are sun-dried or parched by heating in a metal drum. It can be used in soups, stews, stuffings, puddings, or fried rice. Much of what is sold as "wild" rice is actually cultivated and harvested and processed by machine. Hand-harvested lake- and river-grown wild rice is more flavorful than the cultivated variety.

White Rice White rice has the outer mineral- and vitamin-rich bran removed. Refined grains and their products are generally not suitable as staple foods for optimal health, but can be used for variety as occasional supplements to whole grains. Look for white rice that is organically grown and does not contain talc. Organic white rice can be used in making sushi, fried rice, soups, and stews. Like brown rice, white rice comes in short, medium, and long grain varieties. It also comes in "sticky" varieties that clump together when boiled or steamed, such as the "sticky" long grain rice used in Chinese cooking and the Japanese "sticky" short grain rice used in making sushi. Long and medium grain white rices tend toward blandness, and are often used to absorb the flavors of other ingredients in stir-fries, soups, pilafs, stuffings, and other dishes.

Brown Basmati Rice This long grain aromatic rice is grown in India and the United States. The American variety--known as texmati--is grown in Texas. Brown basmati is more nutritious than white basmati, and has a crunchier texture and slightly nutty flavor. It is more suitable for use in semitropical or tropical climates, or for variety in a temperate climate when the weather is hot.

White Basmati Rice Originally from India and Pakistan, white basmati rice has a delicate nutty aroma. When boiled, it expands only in length, not in width, and the grains remain separate. The hybrid basmati grown in Texas is less pungent and aromatic that the native Indian variety. Other Indian rices include sambal, a short grain nonaromatic variety from Sri Lanka and southern India, and gobin ghog, a short grain, aromatic rice grown in North India. Gobin bhog is similar to basmati but with a stickier texture.

Wehani Rice This dark brown long grain rice is grown by Lundberg Farms in northern California. It has a nutty aroma and can be used in stuffings, salads, and pilafs.

Black Japonica This hybrid rice was developed by Lundberg Farms by combining a dark brown medium grain rice with a black Japanese short grain variety. It adds an exotic touch to stuffings, stir-fries, and side dishes.

Red Rice This species of rice, originally from Asia, and now grown in the United States, has a red outer coat. It is suitable for warmer climates or during hot weather, and adds a firm, chewy texture to salads and casseroles. A variety of red rice, known as Sri Lankan Red, has a mild flavor and cooks quickly and is often used with seafood dishes. A short grain variety, known as Lundberg Christmas Rice, has a distinctive nutty, roasted flavor. The grains don't stick together when cooked. It makes nice stuffings, puddings, and desserts.

Thai Rices A variety of rices from Thailand are now available. These include jasmine, a long grain rice with an aroma like that of basmati, Thai sticky, a variety that sticks together when cooked, and sticky black rice. When cooked, this glutinous variety has a dark purple color. People in Thailand use it mostly for desserts.

Italian Rices Rice has been used for centuries in Italian cuisine. The more common varieties include arborio, a translucent rice with a white dot at the center, a highly refined variety known as carnaroli, and maratello, a medium-long partially refined rice that cooks quickly. These rices can be used in risotto and Italian-style soups.

Valencia This variety was introduced to Spain by the Arabs. It is related to the Italian rices and is traditionally used in paella.

Louisiana Rices Speciality rices from Louisiana include wild pecan, a product of the Cajun rice growing area with taste like that of pecans, and della, a hybridized cross between long grain varieties and aromatic basmati.

The recipes that follow introduce the many uses of brown rice, especially the organic short grain brown rice which is most suitable for use in temperate climates. Because of its naturally sweet flavor and chewy texture, rice is the one grain that can be eaten daily in its whole form. And, since it is such a versatile food, it can serve as the basis for an endlessly varied healthful cuisine. As you start cooking with brown rice, I hope you will begin to experience a sense of joy and happiness like that expressed in the following Chinese poem (from the eighth century BC):

We pound the grain, we bale it out.
We sift, we tread,
We wash it--soak, soak;
We boil it all steamy...
As soon as the smell rises
God on high is very pleased:
"What smell is this, so strong and good?"

1
Basic Brown Rice

"Always reflect on the quality of your brown rice and other staple foods, and always seek to improve your cooking. Approach your cooking with a beginner's mind."—Michio Kushi

The quality of water used in cooking has a tremendous effect on the flavor and energy of the dishes you prepare. The best quality water is good, clean well or spring water which is free of chemical pollutants or additives. If well water is not available, good quality spring water can usually be purchased in natural food stores or from spring water companies. Distilled water is lifeless and unnatural, and is not recommended for cooking or drinking.

Usually, a small, two-finger pinch of white sea salt is recommended for each pot of grains. White sea salt is rich in trace minerals. In some cases, a small piece of kombu sea vegetable, which is also rich in minerals, can be used instead. The kombu is first soaked for 3 to 5 minutes and then diced before you place it in the cooking pot. A piece of kombu the size of a postage stamp can be added to each pot of rice that you cook. Sea salt or kombu make whole grain dishes easier to digest.

Prior to washing your grains, beans, seeds, or nuts, first sort them to remove any small stones, clumps of soil, or badly damaged pieces. Place the grains, beans, seeds, or nuts in a bowl, place the bowl in the sink, and fill it with cold water beyond the level of the food. Rinse by stirring gently with your fingers, and pour the water off. Repeat the process again, and

14

then transfer the food, a handful at a time, to a strainer. Rinse quickly under cold water. Your grains, beans, seeds, or nuts are now ready to be cooked or roasted.

To soak whole grains, after washing them in cold water, place them in a bowl or pressure cooker. Add the required amount of water, as instructed in the recipe, and soak, without salt, for 6 to 8 hours. Whole grains can be cooked in the water you use to soak them.

For persons who live in the temperate zones, pressure cooking is the most energizing way to prepare short grain brown rice. It approximates the traditional method in which short grain brown rice was cooked in a heavy pot with a lid made of thick wood. It helps the grains retain energy and nutrients. Pressure cookers are safe and easy to use. Below are several basic methods for cooking brown rice.

Basic Pressure-cooked Brown Rice

This is the most basic method for pressure cooking brown rice. Because the rice is brought up to pressure right away, it has a stronger, more condensed quality of energy. This method is thus more appropriate when stronger energy is needed from your foods.

> **3 cups organic short grain brown rice, washed**
> **4 1/2 cups spring or well water**
> **small pinch of sea salt or piece of kombu, soaked and diced**

Place the washed rice, water, and small pinch of sea salt or kombu in the pressure cooker. Fasten the lid on the cooker and place the cooker over a high flame. When the pressure comes up, place a flame deflector under the cooker and lower the flame. Cook for 45 to 50 minutes.

When the rice is done, remove the cooker from the stove and let the pressure come down. Remove the lid and use a wooden rice paddle to scoop the cooked grain into a serving bowl. Cover with a bamboo mat before serving.

When serving, use the rice paddle to scoop individual portions of brown rice onto each person's plate, or the serving bowl can be passed from person to person and each person can help themselves. Cover leftover rice with a bamboo mat. It can be stored overnight in the pantry or on a kitchen counter.

Quick-soaked Pressure-cooked Brown Rice

This method softens the rice before cooking. The rice cooks more thoroughly and has a naturally sweet taste.

3 cups organic short grain brown rice, washed
4 1/2 cups spring or well water
small pinch of sea salt or piece of kombu, soaked and diced

Place the washed rice in the pressure cooker and add water and kombu (if you are using it in place of salt). Place the uncovered cooker over a low flame until the water just starts to boil. This will take 10 to 15 minutes, depending on the amount of rice in the cooker. If you are using sea salt, add now (but not with kombu), and place the lid on the cooker. Turn the flame to high, and bring up to pressure. Reduce the flame to medium-low, and place a flame deflector under the cooker. Cook for 45 to 50 minutes.

When the rice is done, take the cooker off the burner. Let the rice sit for about 5 minutes. Place a chopstick under the gauge on the lid of the pressure cooker, thus releasing pressure more rapidly. Remove the lid and use a wooden rice paddle to scoop the rice into a wooden serving bowl. Cover with a bamboo sushi mat until you are ready to serve.

Pre-soaked Pressure-cooked Brown Rice

In this method, the rice is soaked from 6 to 8 hours or overnight. Water causes the rice to become expanded and fluffy.

This more expansive quality of brown rice can help balance a dry hot climate or hot summer weather.

3 cups organic short grain brown rice, washed
4 1/2 cups spring or well water
small pinch of sea salt or piece of kombu, soaked and
diced

Place the washed brown rice in a bowl and cover with the amount of water mentioned above. Add kombu at this time if you are using it instead of sea salt. Cover the bowl to prevent dust from entering and set it aside to soak for 6 to 8 hours or overnight.

Place the soaked rice, water used for soaking the rice, and sea salt (if you have not used kombu) in a pressure cooker. Fasten the lid on the cooker and set over a high flame. When the pressure comes up, reduce the flame to medium-low, and place a flame deflector under the cooker. Cook for 45 to 50 minutes.

When the rice is done, remove the cooker from the stove and let it sit for 5 minutes. Let the pressure come down naturally or place a chopstick under the pressure gauge. Remove the lid, and use a wooden rice paddle to scoop the cooked rice into a serving bowl. Cover with a bamboo mat before serving.

Pressure-cooked Roasted Brown Rice

Roasting the grain before you cook it produces a drier, fluffier dish of brown rice. Roasting concentrates energy in the grains, and can be used to help balance humid weather and on special occasions.

3 cups organic short grain brown rice, washed
4 1/2 cups spring or well water
small pinch of sea salt or piece of kombu, soaked and
diced

Heat a stainless steel skillet over a high flame. When hot,

place the washed and drained rice in the skillet. Use a wooden rice paddle or spoon to dry roast the rice, moving it constantly back and forth until most of the water has evaporated. Reduce the flame to medium, and continue roasting for several minutes until the rice releases a nutty fragrance and turns slightly golden. (Be careful not to scorch the grains.)

When the rice has been thoroughly roasted, remove from the skillet and place in a pressure cooker. Add water and sea salt or kombu, and fasten the lid on the cooker. Turn the flame to high, and let the pressure come up. Reduce the flame to medium-low and place a flame deflector under the cooker. Cook for 45 to 50 minutes on a low flame, then remove the cooker from the stove and let the rice sit for 5 minutes. Let the pressure come down and remove the lid. Serve as described above.

Ohsawa Pot Pressure-cooked Brown Rice

The Ohsawa pot is an earthenware pot with an earthenware lid. It is named after George and Lima Ohsawa, who were the founders of the contemporary macrobiotic movement. The washed rice, sea salt or kombu, and usual amount of water are placed in the pot. The lid is fastened on the pot, and the pot itself is placed inside a pressure cooker which has about an inch of water in it. The lid is then fastened on the pressure cooker, and the cooker is placed over a high flame and brought up to pressure. When the pressure comes up, the flame is reduced to low and the rice is allowed to cook for 45 to 50 minutes. This method concentrates energy in the brown rice.

Boiled Brown Rice

Boiling brown rice creates a light, fluffy dish. Boiled rice can be used during the summer or if you live in a hotter climate. It can also be prepared when you desire light, upward energy in your cooking.

3 cups brown rice, washed
6 cups spring or well water
small pinch of sea salt or piece of kombu, soaked and
diced

Place the rice and sea salt (or kombu) in a heavy pot. Cover with a heavy lid. Bring to a boil on a high flame. Reduce the flame to medium-low and simmer for approximately 60 minutes. Remove with a wooden rice paddle and place in a serving dish. Cover with a bamboo mat while waiting to serve.

2
Brown Rice
with Other Grains

"Short-grain brown rice is ideally balanced, particularly for people living in temperate climates. Use a rich variety of staples—rice, buckwheat, wheat, millet, barley, rye, oats, and corn—selecting what grows locally and has been traditionally enjoyed in your part of the world. The grains you eat should be organically grown, free of chemical fertilizer and poisonous spray."—Lima Ohsawa

The usual proportion of rice to other grains in combination dishes is 3/4 to 2/3 brown rice to 1/4 to 1/3 of the other grain. For optimal variety and balance, it is recommended that you combine your rice with other grains on a regular basis. When combining other whole grains with brown rice, it is sometimes necessary to soak, roast, or boil them first.

By combining brown rice with other grains you can create a variety of energies in your primary grain dish, while also providing a variety of different flavors and textures. Some grains, such as whole corn or hato mugi, have a slightly bitter flavor. Other grains, such as fresh sweet corn, sweet brown rice, millet, and whole oats, have a mild, subtly sweet flavor, while others, such as whole barley, wheat, and rye, have a chewier texture. Other grains also add protein, minerals, and other nutrients to your brown rice dishes.

Brown Rice with Barley

Barley has a light, upward quality of energy. Adding it to brown rice makes the dish fluffier and less glutinous. Barley can be cooked with brown rice on a regular basis.

2 cups organic brown rice, washed
1 cup whole barley, washed and soaked for 6 to 8 hours
4 1/2 cups water, including water used to soak barley
small pinch of sea salt or piece of kombu, soaked and
    diced

Place the brown rice, barley, and water in a pressure cooker. If you are using kombu, add now. Place the uncovered cooker over a low flame until the water starts to boil. If you are using sea salt instead of kombu, add it at this time. Cover the cooker, turn the flame to high, and bring up to pressure. Reduce the flame to medium-low and place a flame deflector under the cooker. Cook for 45 to 50 minutes. Remove from the flame, and allow the pressure to come down. Remove the cover and allow to sit for 4 to 5 minutes. Remove the rice and barley from the cooker and place in a serving bowl.

Brown Rice with Pearl Barley

Pearl barley, or *hato mugi*, is valued in Oriental countries for its power to neutralize the harmful effects of animal food. It adds a wonderfully light quality to your brown rice dishes.

2 cups organic brown rice, washed
1 cup organic hato mugi, washed
4 1/2 cups water
small pinch of sea salt or piece of kombu, soaked and
    diced

Place the brown rice, hato mugi, and water in a pressure

cooker. Place the uncovered cooker over a low flame until the water just begins to boil. Add the sea salt, cover, and turn the flame up high. Reduce the flame to medium-low and place a flame deflector under the cooker. Cook for 45 to 50 minutes. Remove the cooker from the flame and let the pressure come down. Remove the cover and let the grains sit for 4 to 5 minutes before placing in a serving bowl.

Brown Rice with Wheat Berries

2 cups organic brown rice, washed
1 cup organic soft spring or pastry wheat berries, washed
4 1/2 cups water
small pinch of sea salt

Heat a stainless steel skillet over a high flame. Add the washed and drained wheat berries. With a wooden spoon or bamboo rice paddle, stir constantly to ensure even roasting and prevent burning. When the wheat berries are done they release a sweet, nutty fragrance, turn slightly golden and may begin to pop. Remove the wheat berries and place in a pressure cooker.

Add the brown rice and water. Mix and place the uncovered pressure cooker over a low flame until the water just begins to boil. Add the sea salt, cover the cooker, and bring up to pressure on a high flame. When the pressure is up, place a flame deflector under the cooker and reduce the flame to medium-low. Cook for 45 to 50 minutes. Remove the cooker from the flame and allow the pressure to come down. Remove the cover and allow the rice and wheat to sit for 4 to 5 minutes. Remove the grains and place in a serving bowl.

Brown Rice with Whole Rye

Whole rye berries can be soaked and cooked with brown rice for a dish with a delightfully chewy texture.

3 1/2 cups organic brown rice, washed
1/2 cup rye, washed and soaked for 6 to 8 hours
4 1/2 cups water, including water used to soak rye
small pinch of sea salt

Place the brown rice, rye, and water in a pressure cooker and mix. Place the uncovered pressure cooker over a low flame until the water just begins to boil. Add the sea salt, cover the cooker, and turn the flame to high. When the pressure is up, reduce the flame to medium-low and place a flame deflector under the cooker. Allow to cook for 45 to 50 minutes. Remove the cooker from the flame and allow the pressure to come down. Remove the cover and allow the rice and rye to sit for 4 to 5 minutes. Remove and place in a serving bowl.

Brown Rice with Whole Oats

Whole oats can either be soaked or dry roasted prior to cooking with brown rice.

3 1/2 cups organic brown rice, washed
1/2 cup whole oats, washed and soaked for 6 to 8 hours
4 1/2 cups water, including water used to soak oats
small pinch of sea salt

Place the brown rice, whole oats, and water in a pressure cooker. Mix and place the uncovered cooker over a low flame until the water begins to boil. Add the sea salt and cover the cooker. Place over a high flame and allow to come to pressure. Reduce the flame to medium-low and place a flame deflector under the cooker. Allow to cook for approximately 45 to 50 minutes. Remove the cooker from the flame and allow the pressure to come down. Remove the cover and allow the rice and oats to sit for 4 to 5 minutes before placing in a serving bowl.

Brown Rice with White Rice

2 cups organic brown rice, washed
1 cup organic white rice, washed
4 cups water
small pinch of sea salt

Place the rice and water in a pressure cooker without the salt or the lid. Place on a low flame until the water just begins to boil. Add the sea salt, cover, and turn the flame up to high. When the pressure comes up, reduce the flame to medium-low. Place a flame deflector under the cooker and cook for 45 to 50 minutes. Remove from the flame and allow the pressure to come down. Remove the lid and let the rice sit for 4 to 5 minutes. Remove the rice and place in a wooden serving bowl.

Brown Rice with Fresh Sweet Corn

Because sweet corn is soft, and not dry and hard like other grains, you do not need to add extra water when cooking it with rice. It adds a delicious sweet flavor to your rice.

3 cups organic brown rice, washed
1 cup fresh sweet corn, removed from the cob
4 1/2 cups water
small pinch of salt

Place the brown rice, sweet corn, and water in a pressure cooker. Add the water and place the uncovered cooker over a low flame just until the water begins to boil. Add the sea salt and place the cover on the cooker. Raise the flame to high and bring up to pressure. When the pressure is up, reduce the flame to medium-low and place a flame deflector under the cooker. Cook for 45 to 50 minutes. Remove the cooker from the flame and allow the pressure to come down. When the pressure is down, remove the cover and allow the rice and corn to sit for 4 to 5 minutes before placing in a serving bowl.

Brown Rice with Sweet Rice

Sweet brown rice is more glutinous than regular brown rice. It adds extra protein, fat, and sweetness to your rice dishes.

> **2 cups organic brown rice, washed**
> **1 cup organic sweet brown rice, washed (for a softer texture, soak for 6 to 8 hours)**
> **4 1/2 cups water, including water used to soak grains**
> **small pinch of sea salt**

Place the brown rice, sweet brown rice, and water in a pressure cooker and mix. Place the uncovered cooker over a low flame just until the water begins to boil. Add the sea salt, cover, and turn the flame to high. When the pressure is up, reduce the flame to medium-low and place a flame deflector under the cooker. Cook for 45 to 50 minutes. Remove from the flame and allow the pressure to come down. Remove the cover and allow the rice and sweet rice to sit for 4 to 5 minutes before placing in a serving bowl.

Long Grain Rice with Millet

Millet was valued in Oriental medicine for its healing properties, especially its beneficial effect on the pancreas. It can be cooked with short, medium, or long grain rice for a variety of flavors and textures.

> **2 1/2 cups organic long grain brown rice, washed**
> **1/2 cup organic millet, washed**
> **6 cups water**
> **small pinch of sea salt**

Place the brown rice, millet, and water in a heavy pot without a cover. Place on a low flame until the water just begins to boil. Add the sea salt, cover, and turn the flame to high. Reduce the flame to medium-low when the water is at a full boil. Place a flame deflector under the pot. Cook for approximately 1 hour. Remove from the flame and place the brown rice and millet in a serving bowl.

Long Grain Rice with Buckwheat

Buckwheat has a strong contractive quality and warming energy. It is delicious when cooked with long grain rice.

2 1/2 cups long grain brown rice, washed
1/2 cup buckwheat groats, washed
6 1/2 cups water
small pinch of sea salt

Place the brown rice, buckwheat, water, and sea salt in a heavy pot. Cover and bring to a boil over a high flame. Reduce the flame to medium-low, place a flame deflector under the pot, and simmer for approximately 1 hour. Remove from the flame and place in a serving bowl.

Brown Rice with Amaranth

Amaranth, a traditional grain from Central America, can be cooked with brown rice for a distinctive taste.

2 1/2 cups organic brown rice, washed
1/2 cup amaranth, washed
4 1/2 cups water
small pinch of sea salt

Place the brown rice, amaranth, and water in an uncovered pressure cooker. Place over a low flame until the water just begins to boil. Add the sea salt, cover and turn the flame to high. When the pressure is up, reduce the flame to medium-low and place a flame deflector under the cooker. Cook for approximately 45 to 50 minutes. Remove from the flame and allow the pressure to come down. Remove the cover and allow the grains to sit for 4 to 5 minutes before serving.

Brown Rice with Wild Rice

Wild rice gives brown rice dishes a delightfully rich flavor. It is especially popular during holidays.

2 cups organic brown rice, washed
1 cup organic wild rice, washed
4 1/2 cups water
small pinch of sea salt

Place the brown rice, wild rice, and water in an uncovered pressure cooker. Place over a low flame until the water just begins to boil. Add the sea salt, cover the cooker, and turn the flame up to high. When the pressure is up, reduce the flame to medium-low and place a flame deflector under the cooker. Cook for approximately 45 to 50 minutes. Remove from the flame and allow the pressure to come down. Remove the cover and allow the rice and wild rice to sit for 4 to 5 minutes before placing in a serving bowl.

Brown Rice with Quinoa

Quinoa was traditionally used in the Andes. It is high in protein and adds extra energy to brown rice dishes.

2 1/2 cups organic brown rice, washed
1/2 cups organic quinoa, washed
4 1/2 cups water
small pinch of sea salt

Place the brown rice, quinoa, water, and sea salt in a pressure cooker. Cover, place on a high flame, and bring up to pressure. Reduce the flame to medium-low and place a flame deflector under the cooker. Cook for approximately 45 to 50 minutes. Remove from the flame and allow the rice and quinoa to sit for 4 to 5 minutes before placing in a serving bowl.

Brown Rice with Sweet Rice and Millet

2 cups organic brown rice, washed
1/2 cup organic sweet brown rice, washed
1/2 cup organic millet, washed
4 1/2 cups water
small pinch of sea salt

Place the brown rice, sweet brown rice, and millet in a pressure cooker and mix thoroughly. Add the water and place the uncovered pressure cooker over a low flame just until the water begins to boil. Add the sea salt, place the cover on the cooker, and turn the flame to high. When the pressure is up, place a flame deflector under the cooker and reduce the flame to medium-low. Simmer for 45 to 50 minutes. Remove the cooker from the flame and allow the pressure to come down. Remove the cover when the pressure is down and place the cooked grain in a wooden serving bowl.

Brown Rice with Whole Oats and Millet

2 cups organic brown rice, washed
1/2 cup organic whole oats, washed and soaked for 6 to
  8 hours
1/2 cup organic millet, washed
4 1/2 cups water, including water used to soak oats
small pinch of sea salt

Place the brown rice, soaked whole oats, and millet in a pressure cooker and mix thoroughly. Add the water used for soaking the oats and fresh water. Place the uncovered pressure cooker over a low flame just until the water begins to boil. Add the sea salt, place the cover on the cooker, and turn the flame up to high. When the pressure is up, reduce the flame to medium-low and place a flame deflector under the cooker. Cook for 45 to 50 minutes. Remove the cooker from the flame and allow the pressure to come down. When the pressure is down, remove the cover. Allow the grain to sit for 4 to 5 minutes before placing in a wooden serving bowl.

Brown Rice with Pearl Barley and Sweet Corn

2 cups organic brown rice, washed
1 cup pearl barley (hato mugi), washed
1 cup sweet corn, removed from the cob
4 1/2 cups water
small pinch of sea salt

Place the brown rice, hato mugi, and fresh sweet corn in a pressure cooker. Add the water and place the uncovered cooker over a low flame until the water just begins to boil. Add the sea salt, cover the cooker, and turn the flame up high. When the pressure is up, reduce the flame to medium-low and place a flame deflector under the cooker. Cook for 45 to 50 minutes. Remove from the flame and allow the pressure to come down. Remove the cover and allow the grain to sit for 4 to 5 minutes before placing in a wooden serving bowl.

Brown Rice with Whole Wheat and Barley

1 1/2 cups organic brown rice, washed
1/2 cup organic whole wheat berries, washed and
**   soaked 6 to 8 hours**
1 cup organic barley, washed and soaked 6 to 8 hours
4 1/2 cups water, including water used to soak grains
small pinch of sea salt

Place the brown rice, wheat berries, and barley in a pressure cooker. Add the water and mix thoroughly. Cover the cooker with a bamboo mat, set aside, and allow to soak 6 to 8 hours or overnight. Remove the bamboo mat. Place the sea salt in the cooker and place the cover on the pressure cooker. Place the pressure cooker over a high flame until the pressure is fully up. Reduce the flame to medium-low and place a flame deflector under the cooker. Cook for 45 to 50 minutes. Remove from the flame and allow the pressure to come down. Remove the cover and allow the grain to sit for 4 to 5 minutes before placing in a wooden serving bowl.

3
Brown Rice with Beans

Cooking brown rice with beans creates a rich, satisfying, and nutritionally complete dish. Because beans usually require longer to cook than grains, they often need advance preparation. They are usually soaked for several hours, roasted in a dry-skillet, or par-boiled for several minutes prior to combining them with brown rice. All beans may be soaked prior to cooking, which makes them softer and easier to digest.

To soak beans, first wash them in cold water, and then place them in a bowl and add enough cold water to cover. Let them soak for 6 to 8 hours. Remove and drain. If you are cooking azuki beans, black soybeans, or chickpeas, you can use the water used for soaking as part of the water measurement. The water used for soaking other beans may be discarded.

Some beans, such as black or yellow soybeans, produce foam when cooked. If you roast them first in a dry skillet, foam will not appear and the beans stay firmer during cooking. This method produces a deliciously sweet dish. If you par-boil the beans for 20 minutes prior to combining them with brown rice, and use the cooking water as part of the final water measurement, this produces a brightly colored dish.

Brown Rice with Azuki Beans

2 cups organic brown rice, washed

1 cup organic azuki beans, washed and soaked 6 to 8 hours
4 1/2 cups water, including water used to soak azuki beans
small pinch of sea salt

Drain the water from the soaked azuki beans and set aside. Place the beans and brown rice in a pressure cooker. Add the water used to soak the beans plus fresh water, according to the amount suggested above. Mix the brown rice and beans. Place the uncovered pressure cooker over a low flame until the water just begins to boil. Add the sea salt, cover, and turn the flame to high. Reduce the flame to medium-low when the pressure is up. Place a flame deflector under the cooker and cook for 45 to 50 minutes. Remove from the flame, allow the pressure to come down, and remove the cover. Allow the rice and beans to sit for 4 to 5 minutes before placing in a wooden serving bowl.

Brown Rice with Black Soybeans

Black soybeans have a thin and delicate skin and need to be washed in a different manner than other beans to prevent the skins from coming off. Take a clean, damp kitchen towel and place the beans in the middle of it. Fold the towel over the beans so that they are completely covered with the towel. Rub the beans with a back and forth, side to side motion. Pour the beans into a bowl. Rinse the towel under cold water to remove soil and dust, and squeeze it out. Place the beans in the towel again and rub as before. Repeat this process one or two more times to completely clean the beans. They are now ready to dry-roast.

2 1/2 cups organic brown rice, washed
1/2 cup organic black soybeans, washed
4 1/2 cups water
small pinch of sea salt

After washing the beans, place them in a strainer to drain. Heat a stainless steel skillet and add the beans. With a wooden spoon or bamboo rice paddle, roast the beans by moving them back and forth and side to side. Start with a high flame, and when the water from washing evaporates, reduce the flame to medium-low. Continue roasting until the skin of the beans becomes very tight and splits slightly, showing a small white streak or split in the skin. Remove the beans from the flame and place them in the pressure cooker. Add the rice and water measurement. Mix the rice and beans. Place the uncovered cooker over a low flame until the water just begins to boil. Place the sea salt in the cooker and place the lid on the cooker. Turn the flame up to high and bring up to pressure. Reduce the flame to medium-low and place a flame deflector under the cooker. Cook for 45 to 50 minutes. Remove the cooker from the flame and allow the pressure to come down. Remove the cover and let the rice and beans sit for 4 to 5 minutes before placing in a wooden serving bowl.

Brown Rice with Kidney Beans

If you par-boil kidney beans prior to combining them with rice, and use the cooking water from the beans, your dish will have an attractive red color.

> 2 1/2 cups organic brown rice, washed
> 1/2 cup organic kidney beans, washed
> 4 1/2 cups water, including cooking water from the
> beans
> small pinch of sea salt

Place the beans in a saucepan, add cold water to cover, and cover the pan. Bring to a boil on a high flame. Reduce the flame to medium-low and simmer for 20 minutes. Remove from the flame and place the beans in a strainer. Drain the cooking liquid and set aside. Place the beans and rice in the pressure cooker and mix. Combine the cooking water with fresh cold water so as to obtain the above water measurement. Place the water in the cooker. Place the uncovered cooker over a low flame until the water just begins to boil. Add the sea salt and place the lid on the cooker. Turn the flame to high and bring up to pressure. Reduce the flame to medium-low and place a flame deflector under the cooker. Cook for 45 to 50 minutes. Remove the cooker from the flame and allow the pressure to come down. Remove the cover and allow the rice and beans to sit for 4 to 5 minutes before placing in a wooden serving bowl.

Brown Rice with Pinto Beans

2 1/2 cups organic brown rice, washed
1/2 cup organic pinto beans, washed and soaked 6 to 8
    hours or overnight, discard water used for soaking
4 1/2 cups water
small pinch of sea salt

Place the brown rice, soaked beans, and water in a pressure cooker. Place the uncovered cooker over a low flame until the water just begins to boil. Add the sea salt and place the cover on the cooker. Turn the flame to high and bring up to pressure. Reduce the flame to medium-low, place a flame deflector under the cooker, and cook for 45 to 50 minutes. Remove from the flame and allow the pressure to come down. Remove the cover and allow the rice and beans to sit for 4 to 5 minutes before placing in a wooden serving bowl.

Chickpea Rice

2 1/2 cups organic brown rice, washed
1/2 cup organic chickpeas, washed and soaked for 6 to 8
    hours or overnight, discard water used for soaking
4 1/2 cups water
small pinch of sea salt

Combine the brown rice and chickpeas in a pressure

cooker. Add the water and place the uncovered cooker over a low flame until the water just begins to boil. Add the sea salt, place the lid on the cooker, and turn the flame up to high. When the pressure is up, reduce the flame to medium-low and place a flame deflector under the cooker. Cook for 45 to 50 minutes. Remove from the flame and allow the pressure to come down. Remove the cover and allow the rice and beans to sit for 4 to 5 minutes before placing in a wooden serving bowl.

Brown Rice with Whole Wheat and Chickpeas

Whole wheat berries add a firm, chewy texture to this dish, while chickpeas provide a rich, satisfying flavor. This dish makes great fried rice if you have leftovers on the following day.

2 cups organic brown rice, washed
1/2 cup organic whole wheat berries, washed, soaked or
dry-roasted, reserve water used for soaking
1/2 cup organic chickpeas, washed and soaked 6 to 8
hours or overnight, discard water used for soaking
4 1/2 cups water, including water used to soak wheat
small pinch of sea salt

Combine the rice, wheat berries, and chickpeas in a pressure cooker and add the water. Place the uncovered cooker over a low flame until the water just begins to boil. Add the sea salt and place the lid on the cooker. Turn the flame to high and bring up to pressure. Reduce the flame to medium-low and cook for 45 to 50 minutes. Remove from the flame and allow the pressure to come down. Remove the lid and allow the rice and beans to sit for 4 to 5 minutes before placing in a wooden serving bowl.

Brown Rice with Lentils

Lentils are low in fat and have a very short cooking time. Simply wash the lentils and combine with brown rice. They will be done at the same time as the rice.

2 1/2 cups organic brown rice, washed
1/2 cup green or brown lentils, washed
4 1/2 cups water
small pinch of sea salt

Place the rice, lentils, and water in a pressure cooker and mix thoroughly. Place the uncovered cooker over a low flame until the water begins to boil. Add the sea salt, place the lid on the cooker, and turn the flame to high. Reduce the flame to medium-low and place a flame deflector under the cooker. Cook for 45 to 50 minutes. Remove from the flame and allow the pressure to come down. Remove the lid and allow the rice and lentils to sit for 4 to 5 minutes before placing in a wooden serving bowl.

Brown Rice with Mung Beans

Most people are familiar with mung beans in their sprouted form. The mung beans themselves can be combined with brown rice.

2 1/2 cups organic brown rice, washed
1/2 cup organic mung beans, washed and soaked 6 to 8
  hours or overnight, discard water used for soaking
4 1/2 cups water
small pinch of sea salt

Mix the rice and beans in a pressure cooker. Add the water and place the uncovered pressure cooker over a low flame until the water just begins to boil. Add the sea salt, place the lid on the cooker, and turn the flame up to high. When the pressure comes up, reduce the flame to medium-low and cook for 45 to 50 minutes. Remove the cooker from the flame and allow the pressure to come down. Remove the lid and allow the rice and beans to sit for 4 to 5 minutes before placing in a wooden serving bowl.

Boiled Brown Rice with Black Turtle Beans

2 1/2 cups organic brown rice, washed
1/2 cup black turtle beans, washed and soaked 6 to 8
    hours or overnight, discard water used for soaking
6 cups water
small pinch of sea salt

Place the rice, beans, and water in a heavy pot. Mix and place the uncovered pot on a low flame until the water begins to boil. Add the sea salt, cover the pot, and reduce the flame to medium-low. Place a flame deflector under the pot and simmer for 60 minutes. Remove from the flame and allow the rice and beans to sit for 4 to 5 minutes before placing in a serving bowl.

Brown Rice with Great Northern Beans

2 1/2 cups organic brown rice, washed
1/2 cup great northern beans, washed and soaked for
    6 to 8 hours or overnight, discard water used for
    soaking
1/2 cup sweet corn, removed from cob
4 1/2 cups water
small pinch of sea salt

Mix the rice, beans, and corn in a pressure cooker. Add the water and place the uncovered cooker over a low flame until the water just begins to boil. Add the sea salt, place the lid on the cooker, and turn the flame up to high. When the pressure is up, reduce the flame to medium-low and place a flame deflector under the cooker. Cook for 45 to 50 minutes. Remove the cooker from the flame and allow the pressure to come down. Remove the lid and allow the rice and beans to sit for 4 to 5 minutes before placing in a wooden serving bowl.

Brown Rice with Black-eyed Peas, Seitan, and Vegetables

2 1/2 cups organic brown rice, washed
1/2 cup organic black-eyed peas, washed and soaked 6
   to 8 hours, discardwater used for soaking
1/4 cup cooked seitan, cubed or diced
2 Tbsp celery, diced
2 Tbsp onion, diced
2 Tbsp carrots, diced
1 Tbsp parsley, minced, for garnish
4 1/2 cups water
small pinch of sea salt

Place all ingredients except the parsley in a pressure cooker. Cover the cooker and place over a high flame. When up to pressure, reduce the flame to medium-low and place a flame deflector under the cooker. Pressure cook for 45 to 50 minutes. Remove from the flame and allow the pressure to come down. When the pressure is down, remove the lid and let the rice and beans sit for 4 to 5 minutes before serving.

Brown Rice with Yellow Soybeans

2 1/2 cups organic brown rice, washed
1/2 cup organic yellow soybeans, washed and drained
4 1/2 cups water
small pinch of sea salt

Heat a dry stainless steel skillet over a high flame. Place

the soybeans in the skillet and roast evenly, by constantly stirring. Reduce the flame to medium-low when the water used to wash the beans has almost evaporated. Continue roasting until the skin of the beans slightly splits. Remove the beans and mix with the rice in a pressure cooker. Add the water and place the uncovered pressure cooker over a low flame until the water begins to boil. Add the sea salt, place the lid on the cooker, and turn the flame to high. When the pressure comes up, reduce the flame to medium-low and place a flame deflector under the cooker. Cook for 45 to 50 minutes. Remove the cooker from the flame and allow the pressure to come down. Remove the lid from the cooker and allow the rice and beans to sit for 4 to 5 minutes before placing in a wooden serving bowl.

4
Brown Rice
Combination Dishes

Brown rice can be combined with a variety of fresh natural ingredients. Combining rice with nuts or seeds, for example, produces a deliciously rich, high-protein dish. Depending on the type of nut or seed you use, you can create dishes with a sweeter or slightly bitter taste, and a more crunchy texture. Beans or vegetables can also be added.

Chestnut Rice

This dish has a delicious flavor and helps satisfy the craving for sweets. Dry-roasting the chestnuts prior to cooking produces a very sweet flavor. It causes the chestnuts to retain a firmer consistency.

> **2 cups organic brown rice, washed**
> **1 cup organic dried chestnuts, washed and drained**
> **4 1/2 cups water**
> **small pinch of sea salt**

Heat a skillet and place the damp chestnuts in it. Dry-roast by stirring with a wooden spoon or bamboo rice paddle, in a back and forth and side to side motion, until the chestnuts become slightly golden in color and release a sweet, nutty fragrance. Place the roasted chestnuts in the pressure cooker. Add the brown rice and water. Mix the chestnuts and rice. Place the uncovered cooker over a low flame until the water just begins to boil. Add the sea salt, place the lid on the cooker, and turn the flame to high. When the pressure is up, reduce the flame to medium-low and place a flame deflector under the cooker. Cook for 45 to 50 minutes. Remove the cooker from the flame and allow the pressure to come down. Remove the lid and allow the rice and chestnuts to sit for 4 to 5 minutes before placing in a wooden serving bowl.

Sweet Brown Rice with Chestnuts

1 1/2 cups organic sweet brown rice, washed
1/2 cup organic dried chestnuts, washed and soaked 3 to 4 hours
3 cups water, including the water used for soaking the chestnuts
small pinch of sea salt

Place the sweet rice, soaked chestnuts, and water in an uncovered pressure cooker. Place over a low flame until the water begins to boil. Add the sea salt, cover, and turn the flame up to high. When the pressure is up, place a flame deflector under the cooker and reduce the flame to medium-low. Cook for 45 minutes. Remove from the flame and allow the pressure to come down. Remove the cover and let sit for 4 to 5 minutes before placing in a serving bowl.

Brown Rice with Almonds

This dish is very nice when served during holidays or on special occasions. It has a slightly crunchy texture and sweet flavor.

2 1/2 cups organic brown rice, washed
1/2 cup organic almonds, washed

4 1/2 cups water
small pinch of sea salt

Place the almonds in a saucepan, cover with cold water, and bring to a boil. Boil for 1 to 2 minutes. Remove from the flame and place the almonds in a strainer to drain. Discard the cooking water. With your thumb and index finger, squeeze the almonds one by one. The skin will come off the almond very easily. Discard the skins. Repeat until all of the skins have been removed.

Combine the par-boiled, skinned almonds with the brown rice in a pressure cooker. Add the water. Place the uncovered pressure cooker over a low flame until the water begins to boil. Add the sea salt, place the lid on the cooker, and turn the flame to high. When the pressure comes up, reduce the flame to medium-low and place a flame deflector under the cooker. Cook for 45 to 50 minutes. Remove the cooker from the flame and allow the pressure to come down. Remove the lid and allow the rice and almonds to sit for 4 to 5 minutes before placing in a wooden serving bowl.

Brown Rice with Roasted Walnuts or Pecans

3 cups organic brown rice, washed
1/2 cup walnuts or pecans, roasted and chopped
4 1/2 cups water
small pinch of sea salt

Place the rice and water in an uncovered pressure cooker. Place over a low flame until the water begins to boil. Add the sea salt, place the lid on the cooker, and turn the flame to high. When the pressure comes up, reduce the flame to medium-low and place a flame deflector under the cooker. Cook for 45 to 50 minutes. Remove from the flame and allow the pressure to come down. Remove the lid and let sit for 4 to 5 minutes before placing in a wooden serving bowl. After placing the rice in a bowl, mix the roasted and chopped nuts thoroughly with the rice.

Brown Rice with Lotus Seeds

In traditional Oriental medicine, lotus seeds were believed to promote strength and longevity.

2 1/2 cups organic brown rice, washed
1/2 cup organic lotus seeds, washed and soaked for 1 to
2 hours, reserve the water used for soaking
4 1/2 cups water, including water used for soaking the
lotus seeds
small pinch of sea salt

Combine the rice and lotus seeds in a pressure cooker. Add water and place the uncovered cooker over a low flame until the water just begins to boil. Add the sea salt, place the lid on the cooker, and turn the flame to high. When the pressure is up, reduce the flame to medium-low, and place a flame deflector under the cooker. Cook for 45 to 50 minutes. Remove from the flame and allow the pressure to come down. Remove the cover and let the rice and lotus seeds sit for 4 to 5 minutes before placing in a wooden serving bowl.

Brown Rice with Sesame Seeds

Either tan or black seeds can be used in this recipe.

3 cups organic brown rice, washed
1/4 cup sesame seeds, washed
4 1/2 cups water
small pinch of sea salt

Mix the rice and sesame seeds in a pressure cooker. Add the water and place the uncovered cooker over a low flame until the water begins to boil. Add the sea salt, place the lid on the cooker, and turn the flame up to high. When the pressure is up, reduce the flame to medium-low and place a flame deflector under the cooker. Cook for 45 to 50 minutes. Remove the cooker from the flame and allow the pressure to come down. Remove the lid and let the rice and sesame seeds sit for 4 to 5 minutes before placing in a wooden serving bowl.

Brown Rice with Pine Nuts

This delicious combination can be enjoyed as a special treat.

> 2 1/2 cups organic brown rice, washed
> 1/2 cup organic pine nuts, washed
> 6 cups water
> small pinch of sea salt

Place the rice and pine nuts in a heavy pot. Mix and add the water. Place the uncovered pot over a low flame until the water comes to a boil. Add the sea salt, cover, and reduce the flame to medium-low. Place a flame deflector under the pot. Cook for 60 minutes. Remove the cover and place the rice and pine nuts in a wooden serving bowl.

Chestnut Rice with Walnuts

> 2 1/2 cups organic brown rice, washed
> 1/2 cup organic dried chestnuts, washed and dry-
>   roasted
> 1/2 cup organic walnuts, washed and coarsely chopped
> 4 1/2 cups water
> small pinch of sea salt

Mix the brown rice, roasted chestnuts, and chopped walnuts in a pressure cooker and add the water. Place the uncovered cooker over a low flame until the water begins to boil. Add the sea salt, place the lid on the cooker, and turn the flame to high. When the pressure is up, reduce the flame to medium-low and place a flame deflector under the cooker.

Cook for 45 to 50 minutes. Remove the cooker from the flame and allow the pressure to come down. Remove the cover and let the rice sit for 4 to 5 minutes before placing in a wooden serving bowl.

Brown Rice with Sunflower Seeds

3 cups organic brown rice, washed
1/2 cup organic sunflower seeds, washed and dry-roasted
4 1/2 cups water
small pinch of sea salt

Place the rice and water in a pressure cooker. Place the uncovered cooker over a low flame until the water begins to boil. Add the sea salt, place the lid on the cooker, and turn the flame to high. When the pressure is up, reduce the flame to medium-low and place a flame deflector under the cooker. Cook for 45 to 50 minutes. Remove from the flame and allow the pressure to come down. Remove the cover and let the rice sit for 4 to 5 minutes before mixing in the roasted sunflower seeds. Remove the rice and seeds and place in a wooden serving bowl.

Brown Rice with Roasted Pumpkin Seeds

3 cups organic brown rice, washed
4 1/4 to 4 1/2 cups water
1/2 cup pumpkin seeds, roasted
small pinch of sea salt

Place the rice and water in a pressure cooker, without the sea salt or the lid. Place over a low flame until the water just begins to boil. Add the sea salt, cover, and turn the flame up to high. When the pressure is up, reduce the flame to medium-low, place a flame deflector under the cooker, and cook for 45 to 50 minutes. Remove from the flame and allow the pressure to come down. Remove the lid and allow the rice to sit for 4 to 5 minutes. Mix the roasted pumpkin seeds in with the rice. Remove the rice and place in a wooden serving bowl.

Baked Brown Rice with Almonds and Vegetables

2 1/2 cups organic brown rice, washed and dry-roasted
1/2 cup organic almonds, washed, blanched, and skins removed
1/4 cup onions, diced
1/4 cup celery, diced
1/4 cup mushrooms, diced
6 cups boiling water
small pinch of sea salt
2 Tbsp parsley, minced

Mix the roasted rice, almonds, onions, celery, and mushrooms and place in a baking dish or casserole. Add the sea salt and water. Cover the baking dish with foil or a tight fitting lid. Preheat the oven to 350 degrees F. Place the covered dish in the oven and bake for 1 hour. Remove from the oven. Remove the foil wrap and mix in the minced parsley. Place in a serving dish.

Black Soybean and Chestnut Rice

2 cups organic brown rice, washed
1/2 cup organic black soybeans, washed and dry-roasted
1/2 cup organic dried chestnuts, washed and dry-roasted
4 1/2 cups water
small pinch of sea salt

Mix the rice, beans, and chestnuts in a pressure cooker and add the water. Place the uncovered cooker over a low flame until the water begins to boil. Add the sea salt, place the lid on the cooker, and turn the flame to high. When the pressure is up, reduce the flame to medium-low and place a flame deflector under the cooker. Cook for 45 to 50 minutes. Remove the cooker from the flame and allow the pressure to come down. Remove the lid and let the rice sit for 4 to 5 minutes before placing in a wooden serving bowl.

Brown Rice with Umeboshi

Umeboshi, or pickled salt plums, give your rice a slightly salty, sour flavor. Since umeboshi are pickled in sea salt, it is not necessary to add salt to this dish.

> **3 cups organic brown rice, washed**
> **1 small umeboshi plum**
> **4 1/2 cups water**

Place the brown rice, umeboshi, and water in a heavy pot, cover, and bring to a boil. Reduce the flame to medium-low, place a flame deflector under the pot and simmer for 1 hour. Remove from the flame. Remove the cover and place the rice in a serving dish.

Brown Rice with Bancha Tea

Brown rice can occasionally be cooked with bancha tea and a small amount of tamari soy sauce (shoyu) for a slightly stronger flavor.

> **3 cups organic brown rice, washed**
> **4 1/2 cups mild bancha twig tea, strained and twigs removed**
> **1 tsp tamari soy sauce**
> **1/4 cup chopped parsley, scallion, or chives, for garnish**

Place the rice in a pressure cooker and add the bancha

tea and tamari soy sauce. Cover the cooker and place over a high flame. Let the pressure come up. Reduce the flame to medium-low and place a flame deflector under the cooker. Cook for 45 to 50 minutes. Remove from the flame and allow the pressure to come down. Remove the lid and let the rice sit for 4 to 5 minutes before mixing in the chopped parsley, scallion, or chives. Place the rice in a serving bowl.

Brown Rice with Dried Shiitake

Dried shiitake mushrooms add a nice light energy to your brown rice dishes.

> 3 cups organic brown rice, washed
> 3 to 4 dried shiitake, soaked for 10 to 15 minutes
> 4 1/2 cups water, including water used for soaking the
> shiitake
> small pinch of sea salt

After soaking the shiitake mushrooms, remove from the bowl, squeeze out the water, and remove the woody tip of the stem with a knife. Dice the shiitake. Place the brown rice, shiitake, and water in a pressure cooker and mix the shiitake evenly with the rice. Place the uncovered cooker over a low flame until the water begins to boil. Add the sea salt, place the lid on the cooker, and turn the flame to high. When the pressure comes up, reduce the flame to medium-low and place a flame deflector under the cooker. Cook for 45 to 50 minutes. Remove from the flame and allow the pressure to come down. Remove the lid and allow the rice and shiitake to sit for 4 to 5 minutes before placing in a serving bowl.

Shiso Rice

Shiso leaves are available in two different varieties: red and green. They are sometimes referred to as "beefsteak leaves" in English. Fresh green shiso leaves can be finely chopped and mixed with cooked rice. Red shiso leaves are found mostly in pickled form or in the form of a delicious powdered condiment. Red shiso is also found in containers of umeboshi plums. The red leaves are used to give umeboshi their characteristic color. To serve them with rice, simply rinse them under cold water to remove salt and chop. They can then be mixed with cooked brown rice.

3 cups organic brown rice, washed
4 1/2 cups water
small pinch of sea salt
1/4 cup red, green, or pickled shiso leaves, finely
minced

Pressure cook the brown rice as described earlier. When it is done and the pressure comes down, remove the lid of the pressure cooker and mix the minced shiso leaves with the rice. Remove the rice and place in a serving bowl.

Brown Rice with Ginger Pickles

Ginger root is used in cooking in many countries around the world. It is available in natural and macrobiotic food stores in pickled form. Rinse the ginger pickles, dice or mince very finely, and mix with rice to give your rice a delicious, mildly pungent and salty flavor.

3 cups organic brown rice, washed
1/4 cup pickled ginger root, finely minced
2 Tbsp minced parsley
4 1/2 cups water
small pinch of sea salt

Place the brown rice, water, and sea salt in a pressure cooker and cook as instructed previously. When the rice is done, mix in the minced pickled ginger and parsley. Place in a serving bowl.

Brown Rice with Pickled Daikon

Takuan, or pickled daikon, aids digestion. It is salty and must be rinsed before chopping and combining with cooked brown rice. Sliced takuan can also be soaked for several minutes to remove salt before chopping and mixing with cooked rice. Be sure to use the naturally processed, organic takuan that is sold in natural food stores.

> 3 cups organic brown rice, washed
> 4 1/2 cups water
> small pinch of sea salt
> 1/3 cup organic takuan pickle, rinsed and finely
>   chopped
> parsley sprigs, for garnish

Place the brown rice, water, and sea salt in a pressure cooker and cook as instructed previously. When the rice is done, mix in the chopped takuan pickle. Place in a serving bowl and garnish with parsley sprigs.

Brown Rice with Fresh Mint

> 3 cups organic brown rice, washed
> 4 1/2 cups water
> small pinch of sea salt
> 1/4 cup fresh mint, washed and finely minced

Cook the rice as instructed previously, either in a pressure cooker or boil in a heavy pot. When the rice is done, mix in the minced mint and place in a serving bowl.

Brown Rice with Squash or Hokkaido Pumpkin

Any kind of hard winter squash, peeled or with the skin left on if the skin is not too tough, may be combined with brown rice to give the dish a delicious, naturally sweet flavor and an attractive orange color. Hokkaido pumpkin, sometimes referred to by the Japanese name *kabocha*, is especially delicious because it is very sweet and stays firm during cooking.

3 cups organic brown rice, washed
1 cup organic winter squash or Hokkaido pumpkin,
sliced into 1 inch cubes
4 1/2 cups water
small pinch of sea salt

Place the brown rice and squash or pumpkin cubes in the pressure cooker. Add the sea salt and water and mix. Cover the cooker and place over a high flame. When the pressure is up, reduce the flame to medium-low and place a flame deflector under the cooker. Cook for 45 to 50 minutes. Remove from the flame and allow the pressure to come down. Remove the cover and gently mix the rice and squash. Let sit in the cooker for 4 to 5 minutes before placing in a serving bowl.

Brown Rice with Watercress

3 cups organic brown rice, washed
4 1/2 cups water
small pinch of sea salt
1/2 cup watercress, washed and finely chopped

Cook the rice as explained previously. When the rice is done, mix the chopped watercress in thoroughly. Remove and place in a serving bowl. The heat of the cooked rice will be sufficient to slightly cook the watercress.

Brown Rice with Parsley, Chives, or Scallions

3 cups organic brown rice, washed
4 1/2 cups water
small pinch of sea salt

1/2 cup finely minced parsley, chives, or scallion

Cook the rice as explained previously. When the rice is done, mix in the minced parsley, chives, or scallion. Remove and place in a serving bowl.

Seitan and Vegetable Gomoku (Mixed Rice)

2 cups organic brown rice, washed and dry-roasted
1 to 2 square inches of kombu, soaked and diced
4 pieces dried tofu, soaked for 10 minutes, diced
1 ear of sweet corn, removed from cob
1/2 cup carrots, diced
1/3 cup seitan, cubed
1 stalk celery, diced
1/4 cup daikon, diced
1/4 cup burdock, diced
3 cups water

Place all ingredients in a pressure cooker and mix thoroughly. Add the water, place the lid on the cooker, and place over a high flame. When the pressure is up, reduce the flame to medium-low and place a flame deflector under the cooker. Cook for 40 to 45 minutes. Remove from the flame and allow the pressure to come down. Remove the cover and let the rice and vegetables sit for 4 to 5 minutes before placing in a serving bowl.

Tempeh and Vegetable Gomoku

2 cups organic brown rice, washed
1/2 cup tempeh, cubed or diced and deep-fried until
   golden
1/4 cup lotus root (fresh or dried), diced
4 to 5 dried shiitake mushrooms, soaked, stems removed, and diced
2 Tbsp dried daikon, rinsed, soaked 10 minutes, and

52

chopped
2 square inches kombu, soaked and diced
1 tsp minced scallion roots
1/4 cup carrots, diced
2 Tbsp scallion, chives, or parsley, minced, for garnish
3 cups water, including the water used for soaking the
shiitake, dried daikon, and kombu

Place all ingredients in a pressure cooker, add water, and mix thoroughly. Place the lid on the cooker and turn the flame to high. When the pressure is up, reduce the flame to medium-low and place a flame deflector under the cooker. Cook for 40 to 45 minutes. Remove from the flame and allow the pressure to come down. Remove the cover and allow the rice and vegetables to sit for 4 to 5 minutes before mixing in the minced scallion, chives, or parsley garnish. Remove and place in a serving bowl.

Tofu and Vegetable Gomoku

2 cups organic brown rice, washed and soaked 6 to 8
hours
1 cup firm style tofu, cubed and deep-fried until golden
brown
1/4 cup fresh sweet corn, removed from the cob
1/4 cup fresh green beans, sliced in 1 inch lengths
1/4 cup carrots, diced
2 Tbsp daikon, diced
2 Tbsp burdock, diced
2 Tbsp celery, diced
2 1/2 to 3 cups water per cup of rice (including the water
used for soaking the rice)
2 square inches kombu, soaked and diced

Place all ingredients in a pressure cooker, add water, and thoroughly mix. Place the lid on the cooker and turn the flame up to high. When the pressure is up, reduce the flame to medium-low and place a flame deflector under the cooker.

Cook for 40 to 45 minutes. Remove from the flame and allow the pressure to come down. Remove the lid and allow the rice and vegetables to sit for 4 to 5 minutes before placing in a serving bowl.

Seafood Gomoku

2 cups organic brown rice, roasted
1/4 cup carrots, diced
2 Tbsp celery, diced
1/4 cup daikon, diced
1/4 cup sweet corn, removed from cob
1 Tbsp minced scallion roots
2 Tbsp burdock, diced
1/2 cup fresh baby clams, washed
1/2 cup fresh small shrimp, shelled and veins removed
1/4 cup fresh mussels, washed
2 Tbsp minced parsley or scallion, for garnish
5 1/2 to 6 cups water
2 square inches kombu, soaked and diced

Place all ingredients, except for the clams, shrimp, and mussels, in a heavy pot. Add the water, mix thoroughly, and cover. Place over a high flame and bring to a boil. Reduce the flame to medium-low, place a flame deflector under the cooker, and simmer for 50 minutes. Remove the cover, place the clams, shrimp, and mussels in the pot and mix gently. Cover and cook for another 7 to 10 minutes. Remove from the flame, place in a serving bowl, and garnish with the minced parsley or scallion.

Tempeh Paella

2 cups organic long grain brown rice, washed and dry-roasted
1 cup tempeh, cubed and deep-fried or pan-fried
1/4 cup onion, diced

1/2 cup mushrooms, diced
2 cloves garlic, minced (onions may be substituted)
1/4 cup green beans, cut into 1 inch lengths
1/4 cup sweet corn, removed from cob
1 Tbsp extra virgin olive or corn oil
4 cups water
small pinch of sea salt
2 Tbsp minced parsley, chives, or scallion, for garnish

Place the oil in a skillet and heat it. Add the garlic and sauté for 1 minute. Add the mushrooms and sauté for 1 to 2 minutes. Place all the ingredients in a heavy pot, except for the garnish. Add the water, mix, and cover. Place over a high flame and bring to a boil. Reduce the flame to medium-low and place a flame deflector under the cooker. Cook for approximately 50 to 55 minutes until the rice is tender and all the liquid has been absorbed. Remove from the flame and remove the cover. Mix in the minced parsley, chives, or scallion and place in a serving bowl.

Seafood and Vegetable Paella

This paella can be served in the pot you use to cook it in. A paella pan, clay nabé pot, or attractive enameled cast iron pot can be used.

2 cups organic long grain brown rice, washed
2 Tbsp extra virgin olive or corn oil
1/4 cup onion, diced
1/2 cup green beans or green peas
1/2 lb medium shrimp, shelled and tails left on
6 small clams, left in shells and washed
6 small mussels, left in shells and washed
2 to 3 cloves garlic, minced
1/2 cup sweet corn, removed from cob
1/4 tsp sea salt
4 cups water
2 Tbsp minced parsley, for garnish

several lemon wedges, for garnish

Place the oil in a skillet and heat. Add the onions and garlic and sauté for 1 to 2 minutes. Place the sautéed vegetables in a heavy pot. Add the rice, green beans or peas, sweet corn, sea salt, and water. Mix, cover, and bring to a boil. Reduce the flame to medium-low and place a flame deflector under the pot. Cook for about 40 minutes. Place the clams, mussels, and shrimp on top of the rice. Cover and cook for another 20 minutes until the rice is done. Remove the cover, garnish with the minced parsley and lemon wedges, and serve from the pan or pot used for cooking the dish.

Brown Rice with Onions and Black Olives

2 cups organic long grain brown rice, washed
2 cups onion, diced
2 to 3 Tbsp corn oil
4 cups water
1 cup pitted black olives, sliced
1 Tbsp parsley, finely chopped, for garnish

Heat the oil in a skillet and add the diced onion. sauté 2 to 3 minutes. Add the rice and sauté for another minute or two. Add the water, cover, and bring to a boil over a high flame. Reduce the flame to medium-low and simmer for 15 to 20 minutes. Add the olives, cover, and continue cooking for another 35 to 40 minutes until the rice is done and all water has been absorbed. Remove the rice and place in a serving dish, gradually mixing in the chopped parsley with each scoop of rice.

Brown Rice with Fresh Shelled Beans

2 cups organic brown rice, washed
4 cups water
1 cup freshly shelled beans (broad, speckle, etc.)

1 tsp fresh dill, finely chopped, for garnish
1 Tbsp fresh parsley, finely chopped, for garnish
small pinch of sea salt

Place the brown rice, beans, and water in a pot. Bring to a boil over a low flame. Add the sea salt, cover, and turn the flame to high. Reduce the flame to medium-low and simmer for 50 to 60 minutes. Mix in the dill and parsley. Remove and place in a serving bowl.

Brown Rice with Deep-fried Tofu and Vegetables

2 cups organic brown rice, washed
1 cup deep-fried tofu, cubed
2 Tbsp bonita (dried fish) flakes
1/2 cup onions, diced
1/4 cup celery, diced
1/4 cup carrots, diced
1/2 cup fresh green peas, boiled until tender
4 cups water
small pinch of sea salt

Place the rice, deep-fried tofu, bonita flakes, onions, celery, carrots, water, and sea salt in a heavy pot. Cover and bring to a boil. Reduce the flame to medium-low and simmer for 50 to 60 minutes. Remove the cover. Mix in the cooked green peas. Remove and place in a serving dish.

5
Rice Balls and Sushi

Rice balls are are easy to make and a great way to use leftover rice. They are wonderful for travel, as brown rice keeps very well when coated with nori and stuffed with umeboshi or pickles. When making rice balls for travel, it is best to use leftover rice rather than warm, fresh rice. Leftover rice will keep longer. Rice balls generally come in four shapes: circles, triangles, spheres, and cylinders. In Japan, rice balls are referred to as *musubi* or *onigiri*. Different types of rice balls are shown in the diagram below.

Umeboshi plum or paste

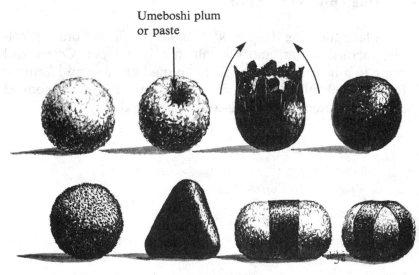

Rice Balls

2 cups (or 2 handfuls) cooked brown rice
1 sheet nori
1 medium umeboshi plum

Roast the nori with the shiny, smooth side up over a flame. Hold it 10 to 12 inches above the flame, and rotate it until the color changes from black to green (about 3 to 5 seconds). Fold the nori in half and tear along the fold. Then fold in half again and tear so that you have 4 equal-sized pieces of nori (about 3-inches square).

Wet your hands slightly in a dish of water. Take half of the rice in your hands and form into a ball, as if your were making a snowball, or into a triangle by cupping your hands into a V shape. Pack the rice to form a solid ball or triangle. Using your index finger, press a hole into the center of the ball, and place half of the umeboshi plum inside. Then pack the rice again to close the hole. Place 1 square of the toasted nori on the rice ball. Wet your hands slightly and press the nori onto the ball so that it sticks. Take another square of toasted nori and place it on the other, uncovered side. Wet your fingers and press the ball again so that the nori sticks. The rice ball should be completely covered with nori.

Repeat until the rice, nori, and umeboshi are used up.

Sesame Rice Balls

2 cups cooked brown rice
1/4 cup tan or black sesame seeds, roasted
1 medium umeboshi plum

Form the rice into two balls or triangles as instructed above. Poke a hole into the center of the rice ball or triangle with your index finger. Place half of the umeboshi plum in each hole. Press the balls with your hands to close the holes.

Roll each ball or triangle in the roasted sesame seeds until completely coated.

Powdered Kombu Rice Bales

2 cups cooked brown rice
1/2 cup tororo kombu (shaved white kombu)

Divide the rice into four equal portions. Shape the rice into cylindrical bales as shown above. Finely chop the tororo kombu. Roll each cylindrical bale in the chopped tororo kombu to completely coat it.

Shiso-leaf Rice Balls

2 cups cooked brown rice
4 shiso leaves (special ones for making rice balls), rinsed

Divide the rice into four equal portions. Mold the rice into circles, triangles, spheres, or cylinders. Take 1 shiso leaf and wrap it around each rice ball and press until it adheres. Repeat until all ingredients are used up.

Pan-fried Azuki Rice Bales

In this recipe, we use leftover brown rice with azuki beans to make delicious deep-fried rice balls.

2 cups cooked brown rice with azuki beans
light or dark sesame oil
tamari soy sauce or shoyu

Form the leftover azuki rice into 4 cylindrical shaped bales. Place a small amount of oil in a skillet and heat. Place the azuki rice bales in the pan and fry until slightly browned on one side. Sprinkle 1 to 2 drops of soy sauce on the rice bales. Turn the rice bales over and pan-fry the other side until slightly browned. Remove and serve.

Pan-fried Rice Balls

2 cups cooked brown rice
2 Tbsp chives or parsley, finely minced
light or dark sesame oil
small amount of pureéd light or mellow miso, pureéd

Mix the chives or parsley with the cooked rice. Form the rice into small or large triangles. Use your fingers to spread the pureéd miso (sparingly, since miso is salty) on both sides of each triangle. Place a small amount of oil in a skillet and heat. Place the triangles in the skillet and fry until slightly browned. Turn the triangles over and brown the other side. Remove and serve.

Deep-fried Rice Balls

2 cups cooked brown rice
light sesame or safflower oil, for deep-frying
1/4 cup tamari soy sauce
1/2 cup water
1 tsp fresh ginger, grated

Form the rice into small balls about the size of a golf ball. Place the oil in a heavy pot suitable for deep-frying. Be sure you have about 2 to 3 inches of oil in the pot. Heat the oil. To test the temperature of the oil, drop a grain of rice in it. If the rice sinks to the bottom and stays there, the oil is not hot enough. When the rice sinks to the bottom and rises to the top almost immediately, the oil is ready to use for deep-frying. Be careful not to let the oil become too hot, otherwise, it will start to smoke. When the oil has reached the correct temperature, drop several rice balls in it and fry until golden. Remove and place on a paper towel to drain.

To make a dipping sauce, place the soy sauce, water, and

ginger in a saucepan and bring almost to a boil. Turn the flame to very low, and simmer 1 to 2 minutes. Pour the dipping sauce in a small bowl or into individual bowls. The rice balls can be placed in the dipping sauce before eating.

Sushi

Sushi is a traditional Japanese dish that has become very popular lately on an international scale. There are many types of sushi. Sushi can be simply a salad of rice and vegetables that is called *chirashi zushi* or *gomoku zushi*. It can be rice with vegetables, pickles, or fish inside rolled in nori and sliced into rounds.This type of sushi is referred to as *nori maki* or *maki zushi*. There can also be maki without nori or with the nori rolled into a spiral on the inside of the roll. Sushi can also be small bales of rice with raw or cooked slices of fish placed on top.

Sushi is a great picnic food. It is wonderful when traveling, and great for special meals or holidays. It is quick and easy to make and can serve as a snack. The best sushi is made from rice that has cooled to room temperature. Leftover rice can also be used. Do not be discouraged if your first attempt at making sushi is a little frustrating and not so attractive. Practice makes perfect. With a little practice, you will be able to make delicious and appetizing sushi.

2 sheets nori, toasted
2 to 3 cups cooked brown rice
1 carrot, cut into 1/4 inch thick lengthwise strips
4 scallions, roots removed
umeboshi paste or umeboshi plums

Step 1: Roast the rough, dull side of a sheet of nori over a high flame, being careful not to burn it, until it turns from a purple, black color to green. Place the sheet of nori, with the smooth shiny side down, on a bamboo sushi mat. Wet both hands with a little cold water and spread 1 to 1 1/2 cups of leftover cooked rice evenly on the nori. Leave about 1/2 to 1 inch of the bottom part of the nori, the part closest to you, uncovered by rice. Similarly, leave about 2 inches at the top of the sheet, the part farthest from you, uncovered by rice.

Step 2: Slice the carrots into lengthwise strips about 8 to 10 inches long and about 1/4 inch thick. Place the strips in a small amount of boiling water, cover, and boil for 1 to 2 minutes. Remove the carrots and place them on a plate to cool. Place the scallions in the same boiling water, cover, and cook 1 minute. Remove and place on the plate with the carrot strips.

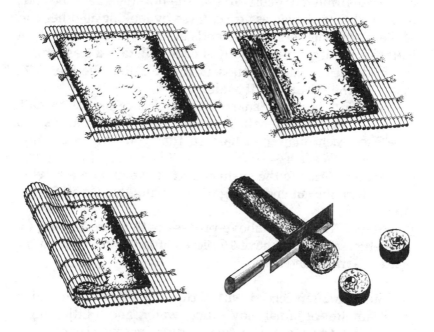

Step 3: Take a small amount of umeboshi paste and spread it evenly across the width of the rice about 1 1/2 to 2 inches from the bottom of the sheet so that it is almost centered on the rice. You can also take small pieces of umeboshi plum and make a line in the same fashion. Use the umeboshi paste moderately, as it is salty. Next, take two carrot strips and lay them on top of the umeboshi paste or plum. Then take two scallions and lay them on top of the carrot strips.

You should now have umeboshi, carrots, and scallions lying in a straight line across the width of the nori.

Step 4: Use the bamboo mat to roll up the rice and nori, pressing firmly against the back of the mat with your thumbs, and tucking and rolling forward with your fingers on the nori and vegetables. Roll up until you are about 1 inch from the top of the nori. Wet your fingers again and moisten the end of the nori across the entire width. Continue to roll into a round log or cylindrical shape. The vegetables should be fairly well centered in the roll. Roll the mat completely around the roll and press firmly but gently to seal the nori together. The ends of the rolls are uneven as you can see by looking at either end of the sushi mat. To make the ends even, so that you get eight equal-sized pieces of sushi out of each roll, take a teaspoon of rice and pack it into the ends of the roll. Remove the sushi mat from the roll and set it aside.

Step 5: Wet a very sharp knife and slice the roll in half. Next, slice each half in half. You will now have 4 quarters of a roll. Slice each quarter in half, so that you have 8 equally-sized pieces of sushi.

Step 6: Arrange the sushi rounds (or maki) on a serving platter with the cut end facing up, showing the rice and vegetables.

Step 7: Repeat the above process with the remaining ingredients, so that you have 16 pieces of maki arranged on the platter. Garnish and serve.

Sushi is often served with a dipping sauce made with a small amount of tamari soy sauce, water, and a little ginger juice or grated daikon. However, a dipping sauce is not really necessary for brown rice (rather than white rice) sushi, or if you are not using fish. Wasabi a hot, green Japanese mustard, is sometimes added to the dip sauce or placed inside the sushi. However, wasabi is not necessary when you are using brown rice and vegetables in your sushi.

Tempeh and Sauerkraut Maki

2 to 3 cups cooked brown rice
2 sheets nori, toasted
1/4 lb tempeh, cut into 1/4 inch thick lengthwise strips
1/4 cup sauerkraut, drained
1/2 tsp natural mustard
4 scallions, roots removed
4 carrot strips, sliced into 1/4 inch thick lengthwise
  strips
2 tsp tan or black sesame seeds, roasted
water
tamari soy sauce
light or dark sesame oil

Place a small amount of oil in a skillet and heat up. Pan-fry the tempeh strips on both sides until golden brown. Add several drops of tamari soy sauce and add water to almost cover the tempeh. Bring to a boil, cover the skillet, and reduce the flame to medium-low. Simmer for 15 to 20 minutes. Remove the cover, turn the flame to high, and cook off all remaining liquid. Remove the tempeh and place on a plate.

Place a small amount of water in a skillet, cover, and bring to a boil. Remove the cover and place the carrot strips in the skillet. Cover and boil for 1 1/2 minutes. Remove and place on the plate with the tempeh. Place the scallions in the same boiling water, cover, and cook for 1 minute. Remove and place on the plate.

Place the nori on the sushi mat as instructed above. Spread the cooked rice on the nori. Take half of the mustard and draw a straight line across the width of the rice so that it is almost in the center of the sheet. Sprinkle half the roasted sesame seeds on top of the mustard. Take half of the tempeh, half of the carrot strips, and half of the scallions, and lay them in a straight line on top of the mustard and sesame seeds. Take half of the sauerkraut and spread it evenly on top of the tempeh and vegetables.

Roll up the sushi as instructed in the previous recipe and

slice into eight equal-sized rounds. Arrange on a platter with the cut end facing up.

Repeat the above process, using all the remaining ingredients.

Tofu and Vegetable Sushi

2 to 3 cups cooked brown rice
2 sheets nori, toasted
1/3 lb firm style tofu, cut into 1/4 inch thick strips, drained
4 carrot strips, cut into 1/4 inch thick lengthwise strips
8 sprigs watercress
several shiso leaves
light sesame or safflower oil, for deep-frying
water
tamari soy sauce
brown rice syrup

Place about 2 inches of oil in a heavy pot for deep-frying and heat. When the oil is hot, place the strips of tofu in the oil and deep-fry until golden brown. Remove the strips and drain on paper towels. Place about 1 inch of water in a saucepan and season with a small amount of tamari soy sauce for a mild salty flavor. Add a small amount of brown rice syrup for a slightly sweet taste. Cover and bring to a boil. Reduce the flame to medium-low and simmer for 10 to 15 minutes. Remove the tofu strips and allow to cool. Squeeze excess liquid from the tofu strips and set on a plate.

Place a small amount of water in a skillet and bring to a boil. Place the carrot strips in the water, cover, and cook for 1 1/2 minutes. Remove and place on the plate with the tofu strips. Place the watercress in the same water and boil for 50 to 60 seconds. Remove and place on the plate.

Place one sheet of toasted nori on a sushi mat. Spread half of the rice on the sheet of nori as instructed previously. Spread half of the carrots, tofu strips, shiso, and watercress evenly in a straight line across the width of the rice so that it is almost centered.

Roll up, slice, and arrange on a platter. Repeat the process again, using all of the remaining ingredients.

Seitan and Vegetable Sushi

2 to 3 cups cooked brown rice
2 sheets nori, toasted
1/2 cup cooked seitan, sliced into strips
1/4 cup sauerkraut, drained
1/2 tsp natural mustard
2 scallions, roots and hard white bases removed

Place the nori on a sushi mat. Spread the rice evenly on the mat as instructed above. Take half of the mustard and spread it evenly across the width of the rice, about 2 inches from the bottom of the sheet. Take half of the sauerkraut and spread it evenly on top of the mustard. Spread half of the seitan strips and one scallion evenly on top of the sauerkraut. Roll up the roll as instructed above and slice into eight pieces. Arrange on a serving platter. Repeat until all of the remaining ingredients have been used.

Cucumber Sushi

2 to 3 cups cooked brown rice
2 sheets nori, toasted
1/4 cup cucumber, sliced into match sticks
1/2 tsp umeboshi paste

Place a sheet of nori on a sushi mat. Spread the rice on the nori as instructed. Take half of the umeboshi paste and spread it evenly, in a straight line, across the width of the rice about 2 inches from the bottom. Place half of the cucumber slices on top of the umeboshi paste. Roll up the roll and cut into eight slices. Arrange on a serving platter. Repeat until all ingredients have been used up.

Natto Sushi

2 to 3 cups cooked brown rice
2 sheets nori, toasted
2 to 3 Tbsp natto (fermented soybeans)
1/2 tsp natural mustard
2 scallions, hard white bases and roots removed
2 to 3 drops tamari soy sauce

Mix the natto, mustard, and soy sauce. Chop the scallions very finely and mix with the natto. Place a sheet of nori on a bamboo sushi mat. Spread the rice on the nori as instructed. Take half of the natto mixture and spread it evenly in a straight line across the width of the rice so that it is almost centered. Roll up the rice and natto, slice, and arrange on a serving platter. Repeat until all of the remaining ingredients have been used.

Daikon Pickle Sushi

2 to 3 cups cooked brown rice
2 sheets nori, toasted
2 strips daikon (takuan) pickle, 8 to 10 inches long by
    1/4 inch wide

Place one sheet of nori on a sushi mat. Spread the rice evenly on the nori as instructed. Take one strip of the takuan pickle and place it in a straight line across the width of the rice so that it is almost centered. Roll up the rice and takuan, slice, and arrange on a serving platter. Repeat until all ingredients have been used.

6
Rice Salads and Stuffings

Brown rice can be combined with other natural ingredients to make light and delicious salads. It can also be combined with vegetables and other foods to make a delicious stuffings. Below are some basic recipe ideas.

Basic Rice Salad

This dish is light and refreshing, and is wonderful during the summer. Most of the ingredients are cooked for only a short time prior to mixing.

4 cups cooked brown rice
1 cup deep-fried tofu, cut into very thin slices
1/2 cup carrots, cut into thin match sticks
1/4 cup burdock, shaved
5 shiitake mushrooms, soaked 10 to 15 minutes and
**   sliced thin**
1/2 cup green string beans, sliced into thin match sticks
1 sheet nori, toasted and cut into thin strips
2 Tbsp tan sesame seeds, toasted
water
tamari soy sauce
sesame oil
rice syrup
lemon juice

Place a small amount of water in a saucepan and bring to a boil. Place the carrot match sticks in the water, cover, and simmer 1 minute. Remove and place on a plate. Place the green beans in the water, cover, and cook for 1 to 1 1/2 minutes. Remove and place on the plate with the carrots, keeping them separate. Place the tofu strips in a saucepan with enough water to just cover. Season the water with a little soy sauce for a mild salt taste. Cover and simmer for 10 minutes, then remove and drain. Place the tofu on a plate with the vegetables.

Place the shiitake in a saucepan with enough water to just cover. Season with a little soy sauce and brown rice syrup for a mild salty-sweet flavor. Simmer for several minutes until all the liquid has evaporated. Remove and place on the plate with the other ingredients. Place a small amount of sesame oil in a skillet and heat. Add the burdock and sauté' for 1 to 2 minutes. Add enough water to half-cover. Cover and simmer for several minutes until tender. Season with a little soy sauce and simmer for another 4 to 5 minutes. Remove and place on the plate with the other ingredients.

Place the fresh cooked rice in a serving bowl. Attractively arrange the vegetables, tofu, and shiitake on top of the rice. Sprinkle the roasted sesame seeds on top. Take 1/2 fresh lemon and squeeze the juice over the vegetable topping. Serve.

Mixed Rice Salad

1 cup organic brown rice, washed
1 cup organic white rice, washed
4 Tbsp brown rice vinegar
3 Tbsp brown rice syrup
small pinch of sea salt
2 1/2 to 2 3/4 cups water
1/4 cup pickled ginger slices, chopped very fine
1 sheet nori, toasted
2 Tbsp tan sesame seeds, toasted
2 Tbsp bonita flakes (optional)

Place the rice, water, and sea salt in a pressure cooker, cover, and bring up to pressure. Reduce the flame to medium-low and place a flame deflector under the cooker. Cook for 45 minutes. Remove from the flame and allow the pressure to come down. Remove the cover and allow the rice to sit for 4 to 5 minutes. Remove the rice and place in a mixing bowl. In a saucepan, heat the brown rice vinegar and rice syrup. Allow to cool. Mix the vinegar and rice syrup mixture in with the cooked rice.

Add the chopped ginger slices, toasted sesame seeds, bonita flakes, and mix. Tear the nori into small pieces and mix with the rice. Place the mixed rice in a serving bowl.

Stuffed Deep-fried Tofu

2 cups cooked brown or brown and white rice
5 slices firm style tofu, sliced in 1/2 inch thick slices, drained
sesame or safflower oil, for deep-frying
1 cup water
1 strip kombu, 2 inches long
3 Tbsp brown rice syrup
2 Tbsp natural mirin (sweet cooking saké)
tamari soy sauce
1/2 cup burdock, sliced into very thin match sticks
1/2 cup carrot, sliced into very thin match sticks
1 1/2 Tbsp black sesame seeds, toasted
sesame oil, for sautéing
3 Tbsp brown rice vinegar

Heat the oil for deep-frying. Place the drained tofu slices in the hot oil and fry until golden brown. Remove and drain on paper towels. Place the tofu in a saucepan with 1 cup water, kombu, brown rice syrup, mirin, and enough tamari soy sauce for a slightly salty flavor. Cover and bring to a boil. Reduce the flame to medium-low and simmer for about 10 minutes. Remove, drain, and allow to cool. Cut the deep-fried tofu slices in half, forming a triangular shape. Take a knife and insert it into the sliced edge of the tofu to open up the triangle. With a spoon, carefully scrape out all of the tofu inside the triangle, so that only the deep-fried shell of the tofu remains.

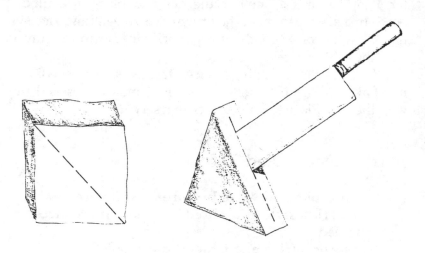

Place a small amount of sesame oil in a skillet and heat. Place the burdock in the skillet and sauté for 2 to 3 minutes. Add enough water to cover the burdock. Lay the carrots on top of the burdock. Cover the skillet and bring to a boil. Reduce the flame to medium-low and simmer for about 7 to 10 minutes until the burdock is tender. Season with several drops of soy sauce, cover, and cook another 3 to 5 minutes. Remove the cover and turn the flame up. Cook off the remaining liquid.

Place the rice in a mixing bowl. Mix the cooked burdock and carrots, roasted sesame seeds, and brown rice vinegar with the rice. Take a small amount of the rice mixture in your hands and form it into a ball or bale as if making a rice ball. Stuff the rice mixture into one triangular slice of the deep-fried tofu. Place on a serving platter. Repeat until all tofu triangles have been stuffed.

Stuffed Cabbage

4 to 6 cabbage leaves, hard stem at base of the leaf removed
2 cups cooked brown rice
1/2 cup seitan or tempeh, finely diced
1/2 cup onion, diced
1/2 cup carrot, diced
1/4 cup celery, diced
1 Tbsp parsley, minced
1 cup sauerkraut
1/2 cup sauerkraut juice
1/2 cup water
1 strip kombu, 3 inches long
tamari soy sauce

Thoroughly mix the rice, seitan or tempeh, onions, carrots, celery, and parsley in a mixing bowl. Shape the grain and vegetable mixture into oblong rounds or bales. Roll the stuffing up inside the cabbage leaves and fasten with a toothpick to hold the rolls together.

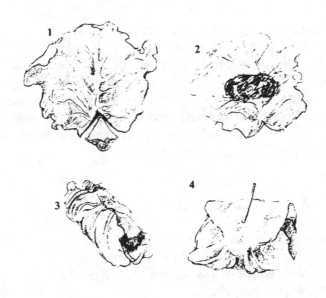

Place the kombu in the bottom of a heavy skillet or shallow pot. Add the sauerkraut juice and water. Place the stuffed cabbage rolls in the skillet. Place the sauerkraut between the rolls. Add a few drops of tamari soy sauce, cover, and bring to a boil. Reduce the flame to low and simmer for 15 to 20 minutes until soft and tender. Remove the toothpicks from the rolls. Arrange the stuffed cabbage and sauerkraut on a serving platter.

Stuffed Mushrooms

10 large stuffing mushrooms, stems removed
1/2 cup cooked brown rice
1/4 cup seitan, finely minced
1 scallion, finely minced
1/4 cup onion, finely minced
2 Tbsp sauerkraut, finely minced
1/4 cup mochi, grated
1 Tbsp parsley, finely minced
tamari soy sauce
sesame oil

Place the rice, seitan, scallion, onion, sauerkraut, and mochi in a mixing bowl. Sprinkle several drops of tamari soy sauce over the mixture. Mix thoroughly. Stuff each mushroom with about 1 tablespoonful of the mixture. Sprinkle with a little minced parsley. Place the stuffed mushrooms in a baking dish, cover the dish and bake at 350 degrees F. for 15 to 20 minutes until tender and the mochi melts in the stuffing. Remove and place on a serving platter.

Baked Stuffed Acorn Squash

1 acorn squash, cut in half, seeds removed
1/2 cup cooked rice and wild rice
1/2 cup whole wheat bread, cubed
1/4 cup onion, diced

1/4 cup celery, diced
2 Tbsp mushrooms, minced
1/4 cup water
tamari soy sauce
corn oil, for sautéing

Place a small amount of corn oil in a skillet and heat. sauté the onions for 1 minute. Add the mushrooms and celery. sauté for another 1 to 2 minutes. Sprinkle 4 to 5 drops of soy sauce over the vegetables. Place the vegetables in a mixing bowl. Add the rice, whole wheat bread, and water. Mix well. Fill each squash half with the stuffing. Place in a baking dish. Cover and bake at 450 degrees F. for about 35 to 40 minutes or until done. Poke with a fork to test. Remove and place on a serving platter.

Stuffed Shiso Leaves

Shiso leaves come pre-packaged in most natural food stores. They can be stuffed and rolled just like grape leaves for a delicious grain dish or snack.

8 to 10 large, fancy shiso leaves, rinsed
1 1/2 to 2 cups cooked brown rice
1/4 cup sunflower seeds, roasted
2 Tbsp chives, scallion, or parsley, finely minced

Place the brown rice, sunflower seeds, and minced chives in a mixing bowl. Mix thoroughly. Take about 1/4 cup of the mixture and form it into oblong rounds like you would if making round-shaped rice bales. Do the same with the remainder of the rice mixture. Wrap or roll the shiso leaves around the stuffing as you would if making stuffed cabbage rolls. Arrange the stuffed shiso leaves on a serving platter.

7
Fried Rice

Fried rice makes a wonderful quick snack. It is a wonderful way to use leftover rice and other foods. The preparation of fried rice can be adjusted to reflect seasonal change. Below are fried rice dishes for each of the seasons, along with ideas for making brown rice burgers and croquettes.

Spring Fried Rice with Wild Vegetables

3 cups cooked brown rice
2 Tbsp sesame oil
1/2 cup chives, finely chopped
1/2 cup dandelions, par-boiled 1 minute, finely
    chopped
1/2 cup burdock, shaved or cut into very thin match
    sticks
tamari soy sauce

Heat the sesame oil in a skillet. Add the burdock and sauté for 1 to 2 minutes. Add the rice, mix, and add several drops of tamari soy sauce. Cover, reduce the flame to low, and cook until the rice is warm. Stir occasionally to cook evenly. Add the chopped chives and dandelions. Stir, cover, and cook for 1 to 2 minutes. Add a little more tamari soy sauce for a mild salt flavor. Cover and cook for another minute or so. Mix and place in a serving dish.

Summer Fried Rice with Sweet Corn

3 cups cooked brown rice
3 ears sweet corn, removed from the cob
1/2 cup green beans or peas, sliced thin
1/4 cup carrots, diced
2 Tbsp sesame seeds, roasted
1 sheet nori, toasted
2 Tbsp sesame oil
tamari soy sauce

Heat the oil in a skillet. Add the rice and sprinkle several drops of soy sauce over it. Place the corn, beans, and carrots on top of the rice. Cover the skillet and reduce the flame to low. Cook until the rice is hot. Mix the rice and vegetables. Add several more drops of soy sauce for a mild taste, mix in the sesame seeds, and cook for another 2 to 3 minutes. Remove and place in a serving dish.

Autumn Fried Rice with Lotus Root

3 cups cooked brown rice
1 cup fresh lotus root, sliced into thin quarters
1/4 cup carrots, sliced into thin quarters
1 cup turnip, mustard, or daikon greens
2 Tbsp dark (roasted) sesame oil
1 tsp ginger juice
tamari soy sauce

Heat the oil in a skillet. Add the lotus root and sauté for 1 to 2 minutes. Place the carrots on top of the lotus root. Place the rice on top of the vegetables. Reduce the flame to low, sprinkle several drops of soy sauce over the rice, and cover. Cook until the vegetables are done and the rice is hot. Stir occasionally. Place the chopped greens on top of the rice and add a few more drops of soy sauce. Cover and cook over a medium flame until the greens are tender but still bright green. Sprinkle the ginger juice over the rice and mix well. Remove and place in a serving dish.

Winter Azuki Fried Rice

> 3 cups cooked brown rice and azuki beans
> 1 sheet nori, toasted and torn into small pieces
> 2 Tbsp tan sesame seeds, roasted
> 1/4 cup onions, diced
> 1/4 cup squash or pumpkin, diced
> 1/2 cup scallion or leeks, finely chopped
> 2 Tbsp dark sesame oil
> 2 to 3 Tbsp water
> tamari soy sauce

Heat the oil in a cast iron skillet. Add the onions and sauté for 1 to 2 minutes. Place the squash or pumpkin and rice on top of the onions. Add several drops of water and several drops of soy sauce. Cover and reduce the flame to low. Steam the rice and vegetables until hot. Remove the cover, and place the scallions or leeks on top of the rice. Add several more drops of soy sauce. Cover and cook 1 to 2 minutes until the scallions or leeks are tender and bright green. Remove the cover, mix in the sesame seeds, and place in a serving dish.

All-season Shrimp Fried Rice

> 3 cups cooked brown and white rice
> 1/2 lb shrimp, shelled, washed, and chopped
> 1/4 cup onions, diced
> 1/4 cup carrots, sliced into match sticks
> 1/2 cup snow peas, sliced in half
> 1 Tbsp sesame oil
> tamari soy sauce

Heat the oil in a skillet. Add the onions and sauté for 1 to 2 minutes. Place the carrots, shrimp, and rice on top of the onions. Sprinkle several drops of soy sauce over the rice. Cover and reduce the flame to low. Cook until the shrimp and vegetables are done and the rice is hot. Place the snow peas on top of the rice and add several more drops of soy sauce. Cover and cook another minute or so until the snow peas are tender but still bright green. Mix and place in a serving dish.

Brown Rice and Vegetable Burgers

4 cups cooked brown rice
2 Tbsp parsley, finely minced
1/2 cup onions, finely diced
1/4 cup carrots, finely diced
1/4 cup celery, finely diced
1/4 cup sesame seeds, toasted
tamari soy sauce
sesame or corn oil, for frying

Place the rice, parsley, onions, carrots, celery, and sesame seeds in a mixing bowl and mix thoroughly. Form the mixture into 4 to 6 burger-shaped patties.

Oil a skillet or griddle and heat. Place the burgers in the hot skillet. Sprinkle 2 to 3 drops of tamari soy sauce on top. Fry until golden brown. Turn the burgers over, sprinkle 2 to 3 drops of tamari soy sauce on the other side, and fry until golden brown. Turn the burgers one more time. Remove and place on a serving platter.

Brown Rice Croquettes with Vegetable-kuzu Sauce

4 cups cooked brown rice
sesame or safflower oil, for deep-frying

Form the cooked rice into 4 to 6 balls or triangles like you would if making rice balls. Heat 2 to 3 inches of oil in a deep-frying pot. Place the rice balls in the hot oil and deep-fry until golden brown. Remove, place on paper towels, and drain the croquettes.

Vegetable-kuzu Sauce

1/2 cup onion, sliced into thick wedges
1/2 cup carrots, sliced into thin diagonals
1 cup broccoli, sliced into flowerettes
1/4 cup celery, sliced into thin diagonals
2 cups water
4 to 5 Tbsp kuzu, diluted in a little cold water
tamari soy sauce
ginger juice

Place the water in a pot, cover, and bring to a boil. Add the onions, carrots, and celery. Cover and boil 1 minute. Add the broccoli, cover, and boil 1 minute. Remove the cover. Add the diluted kuzu, stirring constantly to prevent lumping. When the liquid is thick and translucent, reduce the flame to low and season with several drops of tamari soy sauce for a mild salt flavor. Simmer without a cover for 2 to 3 minutes. Turn the flame off. Squeeze a little fresh ginger juice over the vegetables and mix in. Place 1 to 2 croquettes in each serving bowl. Ladle the vegetable-kuzu sauce over each serving of croquettes and serve.

8
Brown Rice Breakfast Dishes

Brown rice porridges are delicious at breakfast. Breakfast grains are generally cooked with more water than grain dishes served at lunch or dinner. Additional water makes the grains softer and more expanded, and thus more easily digested. A variety of natural seasonings can be used as seasonings or condiments when preparing breakfast porridge, including miso, sea salt, kombu, umeboshi plum, dried fruit, and whole grain sweeteners such as brown rice syrup and barley malt.

Garnishes also balance the energy in your porridges and other dishes. Choosing the right garnish to balance the flavor, texture, and color of your dishes is an important part of cooking.

Soft Rice Porridge

1 cup organic brown rice, washed
5 cups water
small pinch of sea salt or piece of kombu, soaked and
    diced

Place the rice, water, and sea salt or kombu in a pressure cooker. Cover and place on a high flame. Bring up to pressure. Reduce the flame to medium-low and cook for 45 to 50 minutes. Remove from the flame and allow the pressure to come down. Remove the cover and place in individual serving dishes. Garnish with chopped scallion, chives, or parsley, or sprinkle a little of your favorite condiment over each serving.

Boiled Rice Porridge

1 cup organic brown rice, washed
5 cups water
small pinch of sea salt or piece of kombu, soaked and
    diced

Place all ingredients in a heavy pot. Cover and bring to a boil. Reduce the flame to medium-low and simmer for 1 hour. Remove from flame and place in serving bowls. Garnish and serve.

Soft Rice Porridge with Umeboshi

1 cup organic brown rice, washed
1 small to medium umeboshi plum
5 cups water

Place all ingredients in a pressure cooker, cover, and bring up to pressure. Reduce flame to medium-low and simmer for 45 to 50 minutes. Remove from flame and allow the pressure to come down. Remove cover, place in serving bowls, and garnish with toasted nori strips, chopped scallion, and a little gomashio.

Soft Rice Porridge with Pumpkin

1 cup organic brown rice, washed
5 cups water
2 cups Hokkaido pumpkin or buttercup squash, cubed

small pinch of sea salt or piece of kombu, soaked and
diced

Place all ingredients in a pressure cooker, cover, and
bring up to pressure. Reduce the flame to medium-low and
simmer for 45 to 50 minutes. Remove from flame and allow
the pressure to come down. Remove cover and place in serving bowls. Garnish and serve.

Quick Rice Porridge

1 cup leftover brown rice
3 cups water (just to cover rice)

Place rice and water in a pot, cover, and bring to a boil.
Reduce the flame to medium-low and simmer for about 20
minutes until soft and creamy. Place in serving bowls and
serve with your favorite garnish or condiment.

Ojiya

1 cup organic brown rice, washed
5 cups water
1 inch piece of kombu, soaked and diced, add the water
    used for soaking as part of above water measurement
3 to 4 scallion roots, finely minced
3 to 4 scallion tops, thinly sliced
3 to 4 shiitake mushrooms, soaked, stems removed, and
    sliced, add the water used for soaking as part of above
    water measurement
2 level tsp barley miso, pureéd

Place the rice, kombu, shiitake, scallion roots, and water
in a pressure cooker. Cover and bring up to pressure. Reduce
the flame to medium-low and cook for 45 to 50 minutes. Remove from flame and allow pressure to come down. Remove
cover and place uncovered cooker over a low flame. Add the

miso and mix well. Cover cooker with a regular cover (not pressure cooker lid) and simmer, without boiling, for 2 to 3 minutes. Remove cover and place in serving bowls. Garnish with chopped fresh scallion.

Miso Rice Porridge

1 cup organic brown rice, washed
5 cups water
small pinch of sea salt or piece of kombu, soaked and
    diced
3 to 4 shiitake mushrooms, soaked, stems removed, and
    diced, add the water used for soaking as part of above
    liquid measurement
1 cup daikon, quartered and sliced thin
1/4 cup celery, sliced on a thin diagonal
1/2 cup squash, cubed
1/2 cup carrot, diced
1/4 cup cabbage, diced
2 level tsp barley miso, pureéd
chopped scallion, chives, or parsley, for garnish

Place the rice, water, sea salt or kombu and shiitake in a pressure cooker. Cover and bring up to pressure. Reduce flame to medium-low and cook for 45 minutes. Remove from flame and allow pressure to come down. Remove cover. Add the daikon, squash, carrots, and cabbage. Cover with a regular lid, not a pressure cooker lid, and bring to a boil. Reduce the flame to medium-low and simmer several minutes until the vegetables are tender. Reduce the flame to low, add the miso, and mix well. Simmer, without boiling, for 2 to 3 minutes. Place in serving bowls and garnish.

Soft Rice Porridge with Raisins

1 cup leftover brown rice
3 cups water

1/4 cup organic raisins
1/4 cup roasted sunflower or pumpkin seeds, for garnish

Place all ingredients in a pot, cover, and bring to a boil. Reduce the flame to medium-low and simmer for 20 minutes until soft and creamy. Place in serving bowls and garnish with toasted sunflower or pumpkin seeds.

Sweet Rice Porridge with Chestnuts

1 cup organic sweet brown rice, washed
1/2 cup organic dried chestnuts, soaked 3 to 4 hours or
   dry-roasted and soaked 15 minutes, add the water
   used for soaking as part of above water measurement
pinch of sea salt or 1 inch piece of kombu, soaked and
   diced
5 cups water, including water used to soak chestnuts

Place all ingredients in a pressure cooker, cover, and bring up to pressure. Reduce the flame to medium-low and simmer for 45 to 50 minutes. Remove from flame and allow pressure to come down. Remove cover and place in serving bowls. Garnish and serve.

Pan-fried Mochi

In Japan sweet brown rice is cooked and pounded with a wooden pestle to make mochi, a sticky, taffy-like rice cake. Mochi is delicious at breakfast or as a quick, anytime snack. It can be found at most natural food stores.

6 pieces of mochi, 3 inches by 2 inches
tamari soy sauce
chopped scallion, for garnish

Place the mochi in a heated cast iron or heavy stainless

steel skillet. Reduce the flame to low, cover, and brown one side of the mochi. Remove the cover, turn the mochi pieces over, and brown the other side. As the other side is browning, the mochi will puff up slightly. When puffed up and both sides are browned, remove and place on a serving platter. Before eating, sprinkle 1 to 3 drops of tamari soy sauce over the mochi. Garnish with fresh chopped scallion.

Mochi Waffles with Lemon-walnut Syrup

1 lb mochi
1/2 cup brown rice syrup
2 to 3 Tbsp water
1/4 cup walnuts, roasted and finely chopped
2 to 3 tsp lemon juice, to taste

Slice the mochi into quarters, about 3 1/2 inch by 2 1/2 inch by 1/4 inch thick. Place 1 piece of mochi in each section of a dry (do not oil) waffle iron. Cook until puffed up and slightly crispy but not hard and dry. Repeat until all mochi has been cooked. Place on a serving platter. To prepare the topping, place the rice syrup in a saucepan with the water, roasted walnuts, and a little freshly squeezed lemon juice. Place over a medium flame. When the syrup is hot, pour over each waffle.

Mochi Pancakes with Vegetable Filling

1/4 cup onion, diced
1/4 cup mushrooms, sliced thin
1/4 cup carrots, sliced into thin match sticks
1/2 cup cabbage, finely shredded
1/2 cup mung bean sprouts
water
dark sesame oil
1/2 lb plain mochi, coarsely grated
1/2 sheet nori, toasted and cut into thin strips
tamari soy sauce

Brush a small amount of oil in a skillet and heat. sauté the onions for 1 to 2 minutes. Add the mushrooms and sauté 1 minute. Add the carrots, cabbage, and mung bean sprouts. Add enough cold water to just coat the bottom of the skillet. Cover, reduce the flame to medium-low, and simmer for 3 to 4 minutes. Remove the cover, sprinkle several drops of soy sauce over the vegetables, and mix in. Cook 1 minute more. Place the cooked vegetables in a bowl

On a heated, dry pancake griddle, place 1/4 cup coarsely grated mochi, forming a circle or pancake shape. Spread 1 to 2 tablespoonfuls of the sautéed vegetables on top of the mochi. Sprinkle several strips of nori over the vegetables. Next, quickly sprinkle another 1/4 cup grated mochi on top of the vegetables and nori to create a sandwich effect.

By now the bottom layer of the mochi should have melted and browned slightly. Flip the pancake over and brown the other side. The mochi will melt completely, encasing the vegetable filling. Remove and arrange on a serving platter. Repeat until all ingredients have been used. Serve hot.

Mochi Pancakes with Fruit Filling

1/2 lb plain mochi, coarsely grated
1 apple, cored, peeled, and sliced
1 pear, cored, peeled, and sliced

2 Tbsp raisins
1 to 1 1/2 cups apple juice or water
1 to 1 1/2 Tbsp kuzu, diluted
pinch of sea salt

Place the apples, pears, raisins, juice, and sea salt in a saucepan. Cover and bring to a boil. Reduce the flame to medium-low and simmer 3 to 4 minutes until the fruit is tender. Add the kuzu, stirring constantly, until it becomes thick and translucent. Remove from the flame.

On a heated, dry pancake griddle, place 1/4 cup of grated mochi, forming it into a circle like a pancake. Spread 1 to 2 tablespoonfuls of the stewed fruit evenly on top of the mochi. Next, sprinkle another 1/4 cup of grated mochi on top of the stewed fruit. The bottom layer of mochi should now be slightly browned and melted. Flip the pancake over and cook on the other side until browned and the mochi melts. The fruit topping should now be sandwiched between the two layers of melted mochi. Repeat until all ingredients are used. Serve hot. Other fresh or dried fruits may also be used as filling.

Resources

One Peaceful World is an international information network and friendship society devoted to the realization of one healthy, peaceful world. Activities include educational and spiritual tours, assemblies and forums, international food aid and development, and publishing. Membership is $30/year for individuals and $50 for families and includes a subscription to the One Peaceful World Newsletter and a free book from One Peaceful World Press. For further information, contact:

One Peaceful World
Box 10, Becket, MA 01223
(413) 623-2322
Fax (413) 623-8827

The Kushi Institute offers ongoing classes and seminars including cooking classes and workshops presented by Wendy Esko. For information, contact:

Kushi Institute
Box 7, Becket MA 01223
(413) 623-5741
Fax (413) 623-8827

Recommended Reading

Books by Wendy Esko

1. *Aveline Kushi's Wonderful World of Salads* (Japan Publications, 1989).
2. *The Changing Seasons Cookbook* (with Aveline Kushi, Avery Publishing Group, 1985).
3. *Diet for Natural Beauty* (with Aveline Kushi, Japan Publications, 1991).
4. *The Good Morning Macrobiotic Breakfast Book* (with Aveline Kushi, Avery Publishing Group, 1991).
5. *Introducing Macrobiotic Cooking* (Japan Publications, 1978).
6. *The Macrobiotic Cancer Prevention Cookbook* (with Aveline Kushi, Avery Publishing Group, 1988).
7. *Macrobiotic Cooking for Everyone* (with Edward Esko, Japan Publications, 1980).
8. *Macrobiotic Family Favorites* (with Aveline Kushi, Japan Publications, 1987).
9. *Macrobiotic Pregnancy and Care of the Newborn* (with Michio and Aveline Kushi and Edward Esko, Japan Publications, 1984).
10. *The New Pasta Cuisine* (with Aveline Kushi, Japan Publications, 1992).
11. *The Quick and Natural Macrobiotic Cookbook* (with Aveline Kushi, Contemporary Books, 1989).
12. *Raising Healthy Kids* (with Michio and Aveline Kushi and Edward Esko, Avery Publishing Group, 1994).

Books by Other Authors

1. Esko, Edward. *Healing Planet Earth* (One Peaceful World

Press, 1992).

2. Esko, Edward. *Notes from the Boundless Frontier* (One Peaceful World Press, 1992).

3. Esko, Edward. *The Pulse of Life* (One Peaceful World Press, 1994).

4. Faulkner, Hugh. *Physician Heal Thyself* (One Peaceful World Press, 1992).

5. Harris-Bonham, Jack. *Medicine Men: A Play about George Ohsawa* (One Peaceful World Press, 1993).

6. Jack, Alex. *Inspector Ginkgo, The Macrobiotic Detective* (One Peaceful World Press, 1994).

7. Jack, Alex. *Let Food Be Thy Medicine* (One Peaceful World Press, 1994).

8. Jack, Alex. *Out of Thin Air: A Satire on Owls and Ozone, Beef and Biodiversity, Grains and Global Warming* (One Peaceful World Press, 1993).

9. Jack, Gale and Alex. *Amber Waves of Grain: American Macrobiotic Cooking* (Japan Publications, 1992).

10. Kushi, Aveline. *Aveline Kushi's Complete Guide to Macrobiotic Cooking* (with Alex Jack, Warner Books, 1985).

11. Kushi, Michio. *AIDS and Beyond* (with Alex Jack, One Peaceful World Press, 1995).

12. Kushi, Michio. *Basic Home Remedies* (One Peaceful World, 1994).

13. Kushi, Michio. *The Book of Macrobiotics* (with Alex Jack, Japan Publications, revised edition, 1986).

14. Kushi, Michio. *The Cancer-Prevention Diet* (with Alex Jack, St. Martin's Press, 1983; revised and updated edition, 1993).

15. Kushi, Michio. *Diet for a Strong Heart* (with Alex Jack, St. Martin's Press, 1985).

16. Kushi, Michio. *Forgotten Worlds* (with Edward Esko, One Peaceful World Press, 1992).

17. Kushi, Michio. *The Gospel of Peace: Jesus's Teachings of Eternal Truth* (with Alex Jack, Japan Publications, 1992).

18. Kushi, Michio. *Healing Harvest* (with Edward Esko, One Peaceful World Press, 1994).

19. Kushi, Michio. *Holistic Health Through Macrobiotics* (with Edward Esko, Japan Publications, 1993)

20. Kushi, Michio. *Nine Star Ki* (with Edward Esko, One Peaceful World Press, 1991).

21. Kushi, Michio. *One Peaceful World* (with Alex Jack, St. Martin's Press, 1986).

22. Kushi, Michio. *Other Dimensions: Exploring the Unexplained* (with Edward Esko, Avery Publishing Group, 1991).

23. Kushi, Michio. *The Philosopher's Stone* (with Edward Esko, One Peaceful World Press), 1994.

24. Kushi, Michio. *Spiritual Journey* (with Edward Esko, One Peaceful World Press), 1994.

25. Kushi, Michio. *The Teachings of Michio Kushi* (with Edward Esko, One Peaceful World Press, 1993).

26. Lalumiere, Guy. *Macobiotic Home Food Processing*, One Peaceful World Press, 1993).

27. Sudo, Hanai. *Fire, Water, Wind* (One Peaceful World Press, 1992).

About the Author

Wendy Esko teaches macrobiotic ocoking at the Kushi Institute and around the world. She is the author of *Introducing Macrobiotic Cooking*, co-author with Aveline Kushi of *The Changing Seasons Macrobiotic Cookbook*, and author of many other books. She lives with her husband, Edward, a macrobiotic author and teacher, and eight children in Becket, Massachusetts.

Recipe Index

Brown Rice with Parsley, Chives, or Scallions, 51
Brown Rice with Peal Barley, 21
Brown Rice with Pearly Barley and Sweet Corn, 29
Brown Rice with Pickled Daikon, 50
Brown Rice with Pine Nuts, 44
Brown Rice with Pinto Beans, 34
Brown Rice with Quinoa, 27
Brown Rice with Roasted Pumpkin Seeds, 45
Brown Rice with Roasted Walnuts or Pecans, 42
Brown Rice with Sesame Seeds, 43
Brown Rice with Squash or Hokkaido Pumpkin, 50
Brown Rice with Sunflower Seeds, 45
Brown Rice with Sweet Rice and Millet, 28
Brown Rice with Sweet Rice, 25
Brown Rice with Umeboshi, 47
Brown Rice with Watercress, 51
Brown Rice with Wheat Berries, 22
Brown Rice with White Rice, 24
Brown Rice with Whole Oats and Millet, 28
Brown Rice with Whole Oats, 23
Brown Rice with Whole Rye, 22
Brown Rice with Whole Wheat and Barley, 29
Brown Rice with Whole Wheat and Chickpeas, 35
Brown Rice with Wild Rice, 27
Brown Rice with Yellow Soybeans, 38

Chestnut Rice with Walnuts, 44
Chestnut Rice, 40
Chickpea Rice, 34
Cucumber Sushi, 67

Daikon Pickle Sushi, 68
Deep-fried Rice Balls, 61

Long Grain Rice with Buckwheat, 26
Long Grain Rice with Millet, 25

Miso Rice Porridge, 84
Mixed Rice Salad, 70
Mochi Pancakes with Fruit Filling, 87
Mochi Pancakes with Vegetable Filling, 87
Mochi Waffles with Lemon-walnut Syrup, 86

Natto Sushi, 68

Ohsawa Pot Pressure-cooked Brown Rice, 18

Ojiya, 83

Pan-fried Azuki Rice Bales, 60
Pan-fried Mochi, 85
Pan-fried Rice Balls, 61
Powdered Kombu Rice Bales, 60
Pre-soaked Pressure-cooked Brown Rice, 16
Pressure-cooked Roasted Brown Rice, 17

Quick Rice Porridge, 83
Quick-soaked Pressure-cooked Brown Rice, 16

Rice Balls, 59

Seafood and Vegetable Paella, 55
Seafood Gomoku, 54
Seitan and Vegetable Gomoku (Mixed Rice), 52
Seitan and Vegetable Sushi, 67
Sesame Rice Balls, 59
Shiso Rice, 48
Shiso-leaf Rice Balls, 60
Soft Rice Porridge with Pumpkin, 82
Soft Rice Porridge with Raisins, 84
Soft Rice Porridge with Umeboshi, 82
Soft Rice Porridge, 81
Spring Fried Rice with Wild Vegetables, 76
Stuffed Cabbage, 73
Stuffed Deep-fried Tofu, 71
Stuffed Mushroom, 74
Stuffed Shiso Leaves, 75
Summer Fried Rice with Sweet Corn, 77
Sushi, 62
Sweet Brown Rice with Chestnuts, 41
Sweet Rice Porridge with Chestnuts, 85

Tempeh and Sauerkraut Maki, 65
Tempeh and Vegetable Gomoku, 52
Tempeh Paella, 54
Tofu and Vegetable Gomoku, 53
Tofu and Vegetable Sushi, 66

Vegetable-kuzu Sauce, 80

Winter Azuki Fried Rice, 78